This issue of *Ploughshares* is dedicated to

SEAMUS HEANEY
(1939-2013)

PHILIP LEVINE
(1928-2015)

MARK STRAND
(1934-2014)

and

C. K. WILLIAMS
(1936-2015)

PLOUGHSHARES

Spring 2016 • Vol. 42, No. 1

GUEST EDITORS
Alan Shapiro & Tom Sleigh

EDITOR-IN-CHIEF
Ladette Randolph

MANAGING EDITOR
Ellen Duffer

FICTION EDITOR
Ladette Randolph

PRODUCTION MANAGER
Allison Trujillo

EDITORIAL ASSISTANTS
Michelle Betters
& Matt Mullen

DIGITAL PUBL. ASSISTANT
Jessica Arnold

COPY EDITOR
Carol Farash

POETRY EDITOR
John Skoyles

BUSINESS & CIRC. MANAGER
David Weinstein

MARKETING ASSISTANT
Erin Jones

SENIOR READERS
Sarah Banse
& Abby Travis

ePUBLISHING CONSULTANT
John Rodzvilla

ASSOCIATE BLOG EDITOR
Amelia Hassani

INTERNS
Kelsey Aijala, Rachel Cantor,
Kit Haggard & Chloe McAlpin

READERS
Jana Lee Balish | Susannah Clark | Stephanie Cohen | Lindsay D'Andrea
Kristine Grieve | Anne James | Karen Lonzo | Autumn McClintock
William Oppenheimer | Sydney Post | June Rockefeller | Joseph Santaella
Michael Schrimper | Charlotte Seley | Angela Siew | Jordan Stillman | John Taylor

ADVISORY BOARD
DeWitt Henry | Alice Hoffman | Ann Leary
Pam Painter | Janet Silver | Marillyn Zacharis

Ploughshares, a journal of new writing, is guest-edited serially by prominent writers who explore different personal visions, aesthetics, and literary circles. *Ploughshares* is published in April, July, and January at Emerson College: 120 Boylston Street, Boston, MA 02116-4624. Telephone: (617) 824-3757. Web address: pshares.org. E-mail: pshares@pshares.org.

Subscriptions (ISSN 0048-4474): $35 for one year (3 issues and 1 Solos *Omnibus*), $55 for two years (6 issues and 2 Solos *Omnibuses*), and $70 for three years (9 issues and 3 Solos *Omnibuses*); $50 a year for institutions. Add $35 a year for international postage ($15 for Canada and Mexico).

Upcoming: Summer 2016, a prose issue edited by James Wood and Claire Messud, will be published in July 2016. Solos *Omnibus Volume 4* will be published in October 2016. Winter 2016-17, a staff-edited poetry and prose issue, will be published in January 2017. Spring 2017, a poetry and prose issue edited by Jennifer Haigh, will be published in April 2017.

Submissions: The regular reading period is from June 1 to January 15 (postmark and online dates). All submissions sent from January 16 to May 31 will be returned unread. From March 1 to May 15, we also read for our Emerging Writer's Contest. Please see page 209 for editorial and submission policies, or visit our website: pshares.org/submit.

Back-issue, classroom-adoption, and bulk orders may be placed directly through Ploughshares. *Ploughshares* is also available as full-text products from EBSCO, H.W. Wilson, JSTOR, ProQuest, and the Gale Group, and indexed in M.L.A. Bibliography, Humanities International Index, and Book Review Index. The views and opinions expressed in this journal are solely those of the authors. All rights for individual works revert to the authors upon publication. Ploughshares receives support from the National Endowment for the Arts and the Massachusetts Cultural Council.

Retail distribution by Ingram Periodicals, Media Solutions, Ubiquity, and Disticor Direct in Canada. Printed in the U.S.A. by The Sheridan Press.

Seamus Heaney's poem "On the Banks of a Canal" reprinted with permission from Faber & Faber LTD.

© 2016 by Emerson College.   ISBN 978-1-62608-046-1

ISSN 0048-4474

massculturalcouncil.org

MIX
Paper from
responsible sources
FSC® C012947

HONORIFIC

PLOUGHSHARES PATRONS

This nonprofit publication would not be possible without the support of our readers and the generosity of the following individuals and organizations.

CO-PUBLISHERS
Marillyn Zacharis, in memory of Robert E. Courtemanche
The Green Angel Foundation

CONTEST SPONSORS
Hunter C. Bourne III
Denis and Ann Leary

COUNCIL
W. Timothy Carey
Lauren Groff

PATRONS
Carol Davis
Drs. Jay A. and Mary Anne Jackson
Elizabeth R. Rea of the Dungannon Foundation

FRIENDS
Alice Byers
Michael J. and Lynne A. MacWade
Gregory Maguire
James Tilley

ORGANIZATIONS
Emerson College
Massachusetts Cultural Council
National Endowment for the Arts

Co-Publisher: $10,000 for two lifetime subscriptions and acknowledgment in the journal for five years.
Contest Sponsor: $5,000 for two lifetime subscriptions and acknowledgment in the journal for three years.
Council: $3,500 for two lifetime subscriptions and acknowledgment in the journal for three years.
Patron: $1,000 for a lifetime subscription and acknowledgment in the journal for two years.
Friend: $500 for acknowledgment in the journal for one year.

CONTENTS

Spring 2016

Cover: Mark Strand, *Untitled,* 2014, paper collage, 8.25" x 8.5".
Courtesy of Lori Bookstein Fine Art.

ALAN SHAPIRO & TOM SLEIGH
Introduction

When you reach "a certain age," time begins to accelerate, and you become acutely aware that there's much less time ahead than behind. And when your older friends start dying, the closer you were to them, the more their deaths seem impossible, a mistake, some stupid oversight—a fatal lapse of attention that resulted in their slipping overboard when no one was looking.

Homilies and pieties are always offensive when what moved you in a friend was some quirk of speech or character, some physical gesture that becomes expected and welcome, especially in the little rituals of saying goodbye: Mark Strand would always see you to the door and give you a hug. Seamus Heaney would watch you get into a cab and wait on the corner, waving at you until you were out of sight, before turning back toward home. C. K. Williams, when he lived in Paris, always hovered in the doorway in silence for a moment, just to make sure you knew the way to the elevator. And Phil Levine would always be joking as you started down the stairs, the exchange of wit never ceasing until the door closed.

We weren't ready to say goodbye to them, and we still aren't now.

We dedicate this issue of *Ploughshares* to the memory of Mark Strand, Phil Levine, C. K. Williams, and Seamus Heaney. The variety of style, rhetoric, and form embodied by their work, the sense of poetry as simultaneous reckoning with life and language, innovation and tradition, and their paradoxical commitment to imagination as providing both engagement with and refuge from a troubled world— these were the qualities we looked for in the poems we collected. And to make this collection as diverse as possible in its ambitions and achievements, we limited each poet to a single poem. This is our lament for the makers. And of course, what we mean by lament is praise of the highest kind, an affirmation of enduring value.

For the readers who loved their words, for their families and friends, which include many of the poets represented here, we wanted to bring them back—if only in these pages.

ELIZABETH ARNOLD
Diurnal

I had a dream
over and over as a child

in my

shimmering morning-light room,
—it was

set there, where I slept,

woodpeckers hammering at the eaves,
the river's waves' light

moving as if forever on the

far wall.
I'd wake (still asleep) in the dream

—I couldn't speak!—

as the two hands hovered.
So that even if I *thought* I'd say…

(if only to ask—

),
one would, white-gloved, hit

my face (I'd say
slapped

but the

glove ate sound).
I don't remember waking.

L. S. ASEKOFF
Stolen Horses

I am the lion.
I am the keeper of the keys.
Black hats float upon the waters.
When I think, I'm sad; when I don't, I'm elated, over-joyed.
Dazzled by the silverblackbacked mirrorwings of three ravens,
I follow the shadow dancers onto thin ice!

Once I drank silence from a spring,
Once I opened slowly like a flower,
Now my legs are stone.
Once I kissed a dead man in my dreams,
Lay the heart of an ape under my pillow,
Saw the most marvelous things.
Then the doubts began to surface—
Is this island dwarfing or the black swan
Of paleontology? Where in hell
Did these little people come from?
No, it's not easy adopting a wait & see attitude
As words float in the middle of a sentence
Like "a dark till"—& someone cashes in on
Stolen horses or the story of a man with no hands
Who finally learned to play the piano.

The fortune read: *Your infinite capacity for patience
                will be rewarded*
Sooner or later. yet the recovery was slower than expected.
As I waited on the banks for the bailout,
"Pantiless in Hell," a white peacock vogued before me,
Tiara of stars, Moscow snow. "Show me the man,"
The cynic says, "I'll show you the crime."
But I believe "Woman is the world & man lives in it,"
& so gave the performance of my life
Before the robin's egg eye of a robber crow.

PETER BALAKIAN
Stalled in Traffic

under the overpass of the
Cross Bronx, the headlights flash on broken

concrete—between cars and exit ramp—and some
undefined hunk of metal rising out of broken glass;

then the disconnected passage that got us to Manhattan
comes to me like a collage of cities spilling off the map.

All I know is my father left Constantinople
in '22 on a train in the dark snaking into Thrace

and his mother's hand became a trace of history,
a U-turn of collapsing latitudes

as the tracks disappeared into Greece.
By the time they arrived in Vienna
the Prater was hypnotic—a shattered wheel

of glass through which he saw the
Bosphorus sludge and iridescent
petrol from the docks where the caciques

wharfed and the mussel shells poured
like black gems. In the Armenian cemetery
on the Asiatic side, my father stone-rubbed

some dates and names, which burned
like flying dragons in his pocket.

ARI BANIAS
Giant Snowballs

All winter two giant snowballs stood in the center
of the trampled schoolyard, & another one
off to the side I felt bad for, then
felt foolish feeling bad for. Every day
I observed them through the chain link fence.

Three giant snowballs the strewn
parts of a would-be snowperson's body.
I'm trying not to say "snowman"
but we know. He's blank
and numb and separated
so much from himself. The segments of him
roughly equal in size: his head and his trunk and
the lower ball I won't call legs.

Yesterday it snowed,
so today the kids build new ones
all different sizes & blindingly white.
On the snowballs' sides where the sun doesn't shine,
shadows fall, light blue and uncomplicated.

Beside the largest snowball
rests a much smaller one, and I can't help
but see them as mother and child
& wow what a stupid human cultural mess.

Now there are six snowballs and I miss
my old loneliness.

CHARLES BARDES
Plagued by Coleridge

1. Three people walk on a cockle hill: broad-forehead Coleridge, yakking away emphatic whirling his arms; tall Wordsworth keeping his steady measure in long strides; serene Dorothy, taking it in, quiet, melding the men. A farm dog, half-grown, short-legged, snags their scent and runs to accost them, growls a moment, bares his teeth as if to bite, then sniffs them out, nips their ankles, darts off to chase a real or figment rabbit, finally falls in line to follow, trotting behind them for miles, catching their chat, catching burrs, wagging his scruff tail, merry and woeful neglecting his sheep.

2. The poet embarked on a nine-day walk, his staff a broom handle, leaving the husks on the kitchen floor, much annoying his much encumbered wife.

3. My dear wife, nuzzle our children, pay off the butcher, write me direct but
   where

4. How might a bird fly on such a day, wind gusting, spent leaves whirling like mad, tree limbs snap and fall, the pond churns frantic, geese all in a tizzy, the heron willful, stolid and gray.

5. The lad was hungry, rather wanted more than customary porridge and turnips, therefore went with bow by night to hunt and slay the great stag. Roasting such meat, old and young feasted, little brethren sucked the marrow, sweet savor reached the warden who took him manacled to the judge, who found him guilty. Sentenced to transport across waters O transport O hunger O sweet savor Damned poems, would they had left me alone.

6. Sweet sober Quakers, have you not tasted strong ale, sack, nor spirits.

7. which is the poet's metal: iron, brass, silver, lead, gold to airy thinness beat, tin, copper, mercury
     = quicksilver

8. The poet walked for days packing a scant knapsack: tea, brandy, notebook, quills, ink, kerchief, and one spare shirt. Lord he must have stunk.

9. Dorothy wrote: I was melancholy and could not talk but eased my heart by weeping
     —nervous blubbering, says William.

10. As opium undid the poet so did me custom, salary, laundry, and mowing the lawn.

CATHERINE BARNETT

Lyric and Narrative Time at Café Loup

Has it passed quickly or slowly, the young women asked.
A cockroach crawled from the salad and the waiter
swept it with a piece of fresh white bread

into his open hand.
What was it, is it something dead, they asked.
Days go slowly, years quickly is what I could have said.

Szymborska says the most pressing questions are naïve.
For example, who stole the hair from your head?
Who invented all this?

Whenever I see a bald spot I want to shout a little,
in praise. Your mind, who could
have invented such a learned edition?

Such ephemera between my salty legs—
Time is one part of the body that never gets washed.
Think of all the moments between the neurons, is that what they're called?

What's happening?
Tell me again. Soon.
Soon residual noise will be all we make,

and the watch or the watcher ticking overhead
just an ecstasy of quiet, a round opening
through which to see the loud and noisy stars.

MICHAEL BURKARD

Story for Children in Which:

"poor" girl/boy, shoes
shoes catch moonbeams
"because" once upon
the moon near/far side
a shoe factory for
those who'd inhabit
the earth till shoemakers
flourished—and the girl/boy
eventually catch so many
beams they fly to the moon's
side to hover and to
hear this: those who've
been crippled, those who
have not been allowed
to walk this earth
gather in one large
congregation of beams
on a blue night in
mild winter / does dale
ever find his way home,
does Seth believe we are
moved around by giants
manipulated by still
greater giants, does Zac
sing a foreign song,
does Sara still admire
the paintings of Vincente
Von Gauche?

Dry Season at the End of the Empire

Oh yes, the chariots were everywhere that summer.
Running the wide streets and kicking up dust.

No rain for weeks. That's what we all said. No rain.
In drawing rooms. In parlors. At the card table

in The Dowager's Palace, which was just some rooms
she kept at the hotel. Oh, the last days of Empire

when no one quite wants to go home. So dry! All the trees rattling
when the wind blows from the desert. Like bones, she'd say.

Like a dance hall full of skeletons. We played Bridge
at the end of the Empire. The bowls were always full of almonds.

Fields and fields of almonds for us to dip our hands into
and take. Everything growing somewhere. Everything ours.

I am so bored, somebody would say. So bored.
Rattle. Rattle of the ring in the bridge mix. Rattle of leaves outside.

Once, a red bird sat at the window and we all tried to name it
when we knew full well it was a Cardinal.

KATHERINE DAMM
The Middlegame

Tuesday

I'm trying to figure out if you can have two thoughts at once. I mean really think about two things simultaneously, not like be hungry and do math at the same time, which is what I was doing when I originally started wondering in the first place. Focus is my Achilles' heel. Eric figured this out when he first taught me to play, and even though he tells me I need to concentrate, he picks at it when he thinks he might be losing, asking questions he knows will make my mind wander, like *how's Kyle* with a tone, even though he knows I haven't thought about Kyle like that since sixth grade. I've tried to do it: to block out the other thoughts and just see the board the way a computer would see it, big marble pieces sitting on the squares sitting in The Void, but I can't, the other thoughts come in and suddenly I've lost my place. So I figure the next best thing is to be able to think and play at the same time.

So far, I've been able to switch back and forth quickly, which is similar, like how a shirt with red and white stripes thin enough and close enough together looks pink. I'm on auto-pilot right now anyway: the game doesn't start until after the first five moves. There was a period of time where we would just decide on an opening, say, a Sicilian Defense, which I find weird and lopsided, or a Patzer, which is sort of unusual because the queen comes out right away, or my favorite, which is a Ruy Lopez closed. I like it because it gets an offense and a defense started right away, and you can feel out how aggressive your opponent is before anything really happens. We'd just say the opening and set up the board like that to get right into it, and so I could learn the names.

Mom is watching us over the top of *The New York Times Magazine*, but mostly she's just checking her phone. She's fidgeting a lot. She just pulled out her compact for the third time since we started, and I realize that if I were really focused, I wouldn't be noticing those things. Stop looking at mom. Eric has my knight pinned to my king. Move the pawn, threaten the bishop, he retreats; threaten with the second pawn on b4 to kick it away completely. I don't have a plan. Make a plan. Every Move Must Have a Purpose. That's the title of some chess-for-business-people—business-for-chess-people?—book that Eric got for Christmas, since he said maybe he'll study business in college, and half the gifts either of us gets are chess-themed. I do like other things too. I should castle.

We've been here every day this week since Eric's clots are back and they need to keep an eye on him, but he's not even here because of the clots themselves. He's on a ton of anticoagulants and so his blood is so thin that a bruise or cut could start bleeding completely out of control. Weird to be hospitalized because of the treatment, not the disease. Coumadin, 7.5 mg. The yellow dose. I used to call it cow-maiden. People say it sounds scary, and it is when I think too hard about it, but it does also happen a lot. The nurses all know Eric. They know me too, if I'm with him. Two of them say goodbye to him before they leave at the end of their shifts. He's lined his rook to his queen, which is eyeing the e1 square. Pawn to g3, give the king space to breathe. Mom sighs, closes her magazine, and opens it up again right away. I'm not going to snap at her. Eric's other pieces are converging on f2 now, and his strategy is only this obvious when he's about to win. I play it out—two moves from now he'll fork my king and queen with his bishop and there is nothing to do except lose her earlier. He would forfeit now if he were me, which drives me crazy. Play it out.

"I don't feel good about that one, Em. Your head wasn't in it."

Other things Eric does or has done that drive me crazy: even though I beat him almost half the time now, he still talks like he's coaching me. He used to move, leave the room for a snack or the bathroom or something, and then yell out his next move without waiting to see what I did, like he already knew. He nods at the board when he comes up with a strategy and says he doesn't mean to. He talks during the game, and if I don't respond he'll talk to whoever else is in the room. I tell mom not to encourage him. He never pulled this stuff in tournaments, so I know he can help it.

People talk about the idea of a perfect game. Or The Perfect Game. Like the way Eric just ended that one—after a certain number of moves it was inevitable that he would win, unless he intentionally screwed up, because he set up everything so every move I made would eventually result in checkmate, or at least being down a queen. If the perfect game exists, it means that there is some ladder of consequences from move number one that you just need to recognize. It feels like Atlantis or the

Fountain of Youth or El Dorado or something. Like old sailors would say they saw the perfect game at the bottom of the ocean when they almost drowned and everyone else would be like *shut up, you're drunk.*

Almost 5:30, so I leave mom and Eric at the hospital to meet dad at La Cucina. They should both be home by the time I get back. Biking to dinner with dad means that it's spring or he would pick me up in the crisis-mobile, or also he'll drive me if it's raining. Second week this year I've biked over and it's still cold, but it's nice to breathe after the hospital room, not that I mind when I'm in there. Sometimes I'll do homework there for hours without noticing the headache until I leave. The one right now feels as if it should get blown away by the wind. Straightaway by Caruso's and I knead it out left-handed while I steer with the right. Should practice lefty biking.

Dad's waiting out front and he looks old this week. Every time I'm away from my mom for a while, just during summers, I guess, she always looks so old when I see her again, as if she only ages when I'm not looking but makes up for lost time. I see dad once a week, every week, so with him it happens randomly.

I don't open the menu, because I get the chicken parm every time, and when the waiter—who I just call the waiter, but I should really find out his name, since he has our table like every time—sees me, he just says *Diet Coke?* because he knows. Dad pages through the menu and asks "How's Eric?" and I say about the same as Sunday because that's when Dad was there.

"I mean he's bored. And he's bummed he had to miss the game." Eric and I have basically all the same likes and dislikes except sports. "Did you get someone to take the tickets?"

And by the weird, unnecessary apology face he makes before he says, "Yeah, Jennifer and her sister took them," I already know the answer is Jen. It's the only time I see him look awkward.

Jen is dad's new girlfriend. Not new, actually, not new at all. They've been dating for like a year, but I've never met her, although I might have walked in on them on a date once when I went to meet my friends at The Frying Fish and he said he was going out to meet friends of his own. I mean, it was definitely him, but I don't know if the woman was her. I can't quite match up the timeline. The other week when I asked about Jennifer, he told me that he actually calls her Jen and said it like he was letting me in on a secret and not a really common nickname. I try to ask about her so he knows I'm OK with it, and this week I say *how's Jen* instead of *how's Jennifer* so he knows I'm even more comfortable. He's answering but I'm not listening, I'm just thinking about that time I walked in on them on that date. I called Eric after and he said he'd figured. Kyle said parents dating is the worst, but the way he said it made me change the subject to something random about a soap opera we'd watched for Spanish. Smooth move, me. *Un movimiento suave.*

It's good to be here. Dad's a good listener, but when I don't feel like talking, he'll fill the space, and right now I just want to think by myself. I'm seeing if I can listen to him talk about Jen and also play back the game with Eric from earlier. I mostly miss some anecdote about her job, but otherwise I think it's going all right.

Thursday

It's weird they call this Chess Camp since it's twice a week, Monday Thursday Monday Thursday, all year round, which is not what a camp is. Kyle is by the cabinet talking to The Pigeon, who is looking particularly birdlike and bug-eyed today, and I don't want to talk to her, so I say *hi Kyle, hi Alex* and put my stuff at a front desk. She gets so close when she talks that even when she's with someone else on the far side of the room I feel like she's in my space saying dumb things and asking who likes who. It's who likes *whom* anyway, Alex. You are a walking stereotype. Sometimes I think if I were any smarter I would be socially inept. I don't know how Eric does it.

But I'm not any smarter and I might be socially inept anyway. I think about dumb crap all the time. Dumb shit. I looked at pajamas online for three hours yesterday, and it's not like anyone but mom and Eric see my pajamas 95 percent of the time. Or how I wonder if my handwriting makes me look like a lesbian, which I think is what Matt T meant by that comment. Not something a genius would do. Or how I don't even want to play today because I realized my nail polish looks stupid and I'm just picturing my hands moving the pieces with neon green stubs and Kyle's going to call me out on it even though it's just a thing that most girls do. Like how I don't want to date Kyle or anyone really but maybe I'd marry him, which is a long time from now and it's like *oh my gawd, boys.*

I hate when I'm like this.

My old chess coach said he couldn't wait to see what kind of adult

I'd grow into, that I'd have to visit, but the way he said it was creepy, like what's *that* supposed to mean?

Kyle's head is on my shoulder now. He's come up behind me and he's watching me text Anna about our project meeting tonight. I turn the screen off and glare at him because it wasn't secret or important but it might have been. The warmup quiz today is easy stuff, *en passant* capture, my diagram pawns look like obese snowmen; the five instances in which castling is not possible, king can't have moved, rook can't have moved, one cannot castle out of, through, or into check; and what's an absolute pin, which is just a regular pin but to the king.

Kyle and I should probably play other people because we play each other all the time and the whole point of camp is you get to play a bunch of different opponents, but we set up anyway. He beats me the first round and I kind of wish he were a worse sport about it, especially since it went so fast. He's an obnoxiously good sport. It makes me feel like a bitch sometimes. I'm pretty sure we met in a fight back in third grade when my family first got here, which means I probably fought and he was probably cool about it. Most friends I made as a kid I had a fight with first. In nursery school I bit Amelia and then she was my best friend until we moved up here. We talk online every once in a while and she says when people ask, she still tells them that she's so weird because I bit her and passed it on like a disease.

I'm not that weird anymore, though, I don't think. I used to be way more hyper and annoying, but being sad a couple years ago kind of had a nice side effect of calming me down. Maybe that just happens to everyone when they get older, regardless.

Our moms are probably out getting coffee at Beanie's right now. They hang out while we're at camp, which is cute because we can take credit for their friendship. I wonder what it's like for adults to be friends. I get the sense it entails a lot of complaining. A long, long time ago, I overheard his mom out in the lobby saying to my mom how great it's been for Kyle to have me as a friend, which made me feel bad because the way she said it was like he didn't have friends when he was little, probably because everyone else sucked. And really liked playing sports. I guess if I didn't have him, or Amelia back in the day, I wouldn't have had any friends except Eric, who's way older than me. That's a new thought. And it's a pretty sad one. Or maybe not, because it worked out OK, All's Well That Ends Well. I almost wouldn't mind if Kyle had a few less friends now. I don't know what I would do if he got Too Cool next year. Not that I actually think he would, but I've been told people change, and the high school is huge.

I can take a good look at him whenever it's his turn and he's focused on the board. It seems as if he's found a move but is checking for a better one. He's getting better-looking, not as in I personally am attracted to him, blah blah blah, but as in objectively things are going to get different for him. I'm trying to do one of those time-lapse aging things. The sleazy-looking mustache shadow he gets every couple of weeks is back, and he must be proud of it because otherwise he would get rid of it right away like I tell him to. Trash-stache. Thankfully, he still has braces and stupid too-long hair, but he's starting to get a real jawline, so it's only a matter of time. I kind of hate that someday he might have a girlfriend who thinks he's always been cool and doesn't even know that he legitimately peed himself while laughing as little as two years ago. To be fair that was shortly after Eric paid him ten dollars to chug a gallon of apple juice, but come on, get it together, the bathroom was right there. And it's not like he actually had to drink all that. I turned the ten dollars down.

My parents used to tease me about Kyle, but by now they've stopped and only Eric does every once in a while. Although mom did super awkwardly ask me last year if I had "romantic feelings" for him or about him or something and I was like Dear Lord in Heaven please let me die before this conversation continues. Mom is really fantastic at approaching these heart-to-hearts in the most uncomfortable way possible. We watched a video in Physics about scientists who are trying to build empathetic robots and it kind of reminded me of my mom when she tries too hard to be cool about stuff. The other day out of nowhere she asked me if people in my class are having oral sex, which I guess maybe people like Kelly are, or at least that's what people say, but really, Mom, that is so far from my reality right now. You clearly think I'm a lot cooler than I am. I didn't say that, I just said *MOTHER* and stared at her until she apologized and said that she was just asking. I told her she watches too much TV.

And she wasn't "just asking" if people in my class were. She was asking if *I* was. Hah. Hah hah.

I can successfully conclude it's a rousing failure to play without paying attention at all. Kyle asks what's up, like why am I playing so badly, and

I say Eric's back in the hospital as usual, which isn't even what I was thinking about.

I hate losing, and I hate losing to Kyle more than anyone. He only started playing chess because I did. I guess I only started because Eric did. The other pairs are still playing, so we quick set up a new game before we have to switch. If Eric had seen that last game he would say in a really patronizing way that I need to get back to the principles, which are especially good to remember when you don't have a strategy. Principles aren't rules—rules are rules. They're more like common sense. The basics of good play. Obviously if you see something better than a common-sense move, you should do that, but if you don't have anything, then you should do stuff like safeguard the king, develop pieces, energize your pawn structure. Sounds New Age. Don't think about the endgame, whenever that is, just wait for an error. A lot of chess is just waiting for the other person to screw up, so if you don't know what else to do, it's a good idea to focus on not screwing up. That sounds obvious but people forget all the time when they try to play aggressively.

The way I see the board is like four quadrants, obviously four if they're quadrants, and the pieces move into each of the quadrants like gathering clouds. My phone buzzes in my pocket, but I'm about to figure something out. Attacks are like storms, then, and you just keep an eye out for the storms, try to make some of your own, and if you see one of theirs, break it up. I'm trying to look at the board like that when I see it, but more than see it, and it seems ridiculous to even think this, I feel it. The game hasn't even started yet, but when it does, the moves are coming and my hand is making them before I even calculate. Pawn to d4, not usually recommended to introduce a third pawn into an opening, but it makes sense, or at least will make sense later. The buzzing of the phone even seems to help. Pressure on the base point and his whole pawn line comes down like dominoes. It feels as if Kyle is far away or underwater. His pieces are small, maybe annoying but that's it, like my hands are huge and I'm swatting them away. I completely have control of the center at this point and everything is just being pushed outward—it's just a matter of time but there's no question that I'll win. And checkmate.

After every game, I've started going through the moves, retracing and analyzing every step. If it was a particularly good one, I play it back and log the steps in my notebook, but I don't think I could do that with this one. I can barely remember past the move-six exchange. Kyle reaches out to shake my hand, but I ignore it because I feel annoyed at him even though he hasn't done anything really, don't even look at him, instead pull my phone out—buzzing the whole time?—six missed calls from mom, two from dad.

It's surreal to see my parents standing next to one another in the waiting room, like meeting someone you only ever saw as a baby. A place in the back of my head is glad to see them together, but I can't think about that now, or at all, because them together means something terrible has happened.

Mom is talking but she hasn't said whether he's OK or not. "He looks very scary, so you don't have to if you don't want to." I'm nodding. I don't know what's being asked of me, but if I could just see him for myself because no one is being clear about what anything means.

Dad opens the door for me and mom hangs back by the plastic chairs. She's standing like a little sister. She's shorter than me now. I forget sometimes that she has it too, and then I'm in the room.

"Hi Eric."

My face feels lopsided from crying and nose running, a screwed-up mirror image of his, both of us melting like clocks. The Dalí poster in Miss Moreno's classroom, above the chalkboard. His face is grotesque, but like he could stop if he wanted to, fix his mouth, quit that surreal half wink. We're so ugly right now. It's an ugly painting.

"I don't know if you can hear me. Mom said to just talk." His eyes are skewed. I can't tell if he's looking at me or if that's just how his head is positioned. "So, this will sound crazy, but I think I played a perfect game today." Maybe he doesn't see anything. Maybe he's seeing two of everything.

"I broke like four rules to do it. I played the opening like the middlegame. My first three moves were all pawns. I brought my queen out really early. I let him double my pawns in two different piece trades. I didn't castle. Like at all. And I could have."

Stupid. No different than a description of any unlikely win.

"When you win a normal game you can look back and see why all of your moves were the right move to make. I had that from the beginning this time. Like when you win, you could have made a wrong move, but you didn't. For this one I *couldn't* make a wrong move in the first place. That's the perfect game, isn't it?"

There's drool on the side of his chin and I feel like I'm supposed to wipe it off. I don't want to touch him. I try to figure out if the sheets are white or light light blue. Light light blue, probably, but I'll have to check in the daylight. I might not be in this room again in the daylight. Think about something else.

"It was against Kyle. Please don't make a big deal out of that. Or do. If you can say something please say something. But if you snap out of this just to make fun of me about Kyle, you're an asshole." Jesus Christ if the last thing I say to my brother is that he's an asshole. "I love you."

Dad's hand is on my shoulder and we're leaving the room while a nurse comes in. I think it's Vanessa.

Friday

Dr. Isaacson explains that Transient Ischemic Attack is due to a blood clot in the brain—actually arterial. It looks like a stroke and then resolves, no brain damage or anything. Even a doctor can't tell the difference between a stroke and a TIA—the acronym is Spanish for aunt, all caps, so Eric and I have been calling it *AUNT!*—until it passes. Patients experience left- or right-sided paralysis, a droop of the side of the face, and loss of speech. Sometimes the gaze can be directed in one direction or another, and the patient can "neglect" the affected side. And then it's gone. Mom wrote it all down and I copied it into my notebook. The technical language looks automatically juvenile in my handwriting. I might as well dot the i's with hearts.

Thirty-six more hours here because an *AUNT!* can be a signal for a real stroke, especially in the first forty-eight hours after it. Mom's letting me skip school and we're playing to pass the time. Eric looks exhausted and he's losing every game, but I don't think either of us wants to talk, so we just keep resetting the board and going again. Factor-five-leiden. It's genetic but it probably would have showed up already if I had it too. It looks like a court case on paper. Factor V Leiden: Factor-plaintiff and Leiden-defendant. Familiar, but the *AUNT!* is new. For Eric—I think mom had one a long time ago, but I don't want to ask. I think I'm supposed to already know.

"So you played the perfect game with Kyle, huh? What do you think that means?"

When he smiles the bags under his eyes lift up and his skin doesn't look so ashy. This is the first time I've looked him straight in the face and it's like when you remind yourself that a nightmare was just a dream, which is especially hard when it took place in some version of your bedroom.

"I wasn't going to trade queens, but now I am. That's what it means."

"Aggressive. Unnecessary."

If they bring a cot for me I'll stay overnight. Eric looks like he's about to fall asleep, but he must be all right because he's beating me. Equal pieces but he's got a better influence on the center. And he's being a jerk about it. I use a trick for when I'm stuck, visualizing the board from the other side, rotate it in my head. Everything changes even though nothing moves. Like how I think of Eric as a brother even though from another side he's a son. Mom and dad are trading shifts. The hospital headache is somewhere in the back of my head, but mostly I just feel happy, which doesn't make any sense. I pin the c pawn to his king and try to get control of the d file. If I constrain just one of his pieces, maybe I can turn this around.

PETER CAMPION

For My Teacher on His Ninetieth Birthday

Birds on a limb
so far as we know
sing no early
bird elegies.
So
        bird on a limb
‚here's no grim gift
but low squawked
hackle trembling
antiphony
to your lines
about the birds
not knowing
who in the trees
they're singing for
yet startling
the world awake
so that the rains
and air and stones
seem things their bird
cries make:
           those lines
make me remember
how one poet
told "there lived
ten thousand
Agamemnons
before Agamemnon:
night blooming jasmine
blistering off
the same one stem.
But no one ever
(since no poet

wrote this for us)
cried for them."

To Wait and Not Yearn for the Waiting to End

The day's wait over, empty-handed, I head for the truck.
Some hunting days are like this, big sky showing itself off,
blue down through purple to orange, salmon clouds.

I'm recalling the lichen-shagged dead maple snag
I stared at for an hour from my tree stand,
green and gray and white starbursts, feathery at the edges,

something new being made of the old tree.
You could almost see the work being done, the becoming.
I was being still with more stillness to come,

plenty of time to think of the man who taught me to hunt,
pale, white on white in the hospital bed, something at work there too,
plenty of time to think and then plenty of time not to think,

hours in the stand, swaying with the tree in the breeze.
Done, I prop against the truck's quarter panel and wait, still being still,
still being, empty-handed enough to notice something working the sky.

ANDREA COHEN
Task Lighting

The miner's lamp brightens
dark truths, what we already

knew: the working man never
has enough hands or eyes.

The candle in the garment
district flickers, then goes out

the third-floor window on the skirts
of a girl from Lawrence, Mass.

Actual wattage may vary,
depending on flames and

incandescence, on the trajectory
of men descending and women

falling. There's a task for every
light. It's the right sun rising

and settling on the dimness
of tenements we've yet to invent.

MICHAEL COLLIER
A Wild Tom Turkey

When he's in the yard he's hard to find
not like when he stands in the stubble
across the road brewing his voice

with deeper and deeper percolations
of what sounds like, "I'll fuck anything
in feathers," stopping now and then

to display his fan and perform a wobbly
polka, chest heavy as he breasts forward
but never closing on the hens who stay

in wary steps ahead conversing only
with themselves, their spindly heads foraging,
measuring the distance that frustrates

his occasional flustering leaps so that
when they reach the street, their scurry
encourages him to fly, as if he's both

bull and matador, charging and turning
in the air but landing in a bounding
forward heap and the whole rafter

of them disappears into the grass,
where after much silence, after the sun
rises and sets and rises, after commandments

come down from mountains, after armistices
and treaties are written what happens
unseen in the grass still sounds like murder.

C. L. DALLAT

How It Was

When he came back he wanted it all
to have been the whiff of Gitanes,
Place du Tertre silhouettes, *carnets*
de billets, and the Clignancourt jazzers
but in truth it was neither
the city nor the heart-stopping
Hovercraft ride but the long dark
night of the North, the Artois,
and L'Île de France, where they'd stared out
every few leagues at something they'd never
seen before, genuine Pinocchio
fairgrounds of incandescence
au bord de l'Autoroute. Later
they would tire of service areas
even those in *Pays Bas* or Austria: anyway
their coach driver, took them off-road
to an old-fashioned tavern
by the serried ranks of Arras
where they drank smaller coffees
than they'd ever seen, under the
baleful gaze of two black wolves
and embarked gratefully
for the kilometres ahead,
her sleeping, ruby-ringed hands in his.

SUSAN DAVIS
Babushkas

Stalin's genocide might never have happened in Pripyat, just outside
    Chernobyl,
where soldiers told her father who asked to keep a few potatoes,
Your soul will fly away and we'll wrap your guts around the phone wires.
Her family nearly killed and ate her. Then came the Germans—

posing in *lederhosen* on the terrace walls of Hitler's
Edelweiss—the pure white flower of the Mother- or Fatherland, inedible.
Fathers and mothers of whom? Goebbel's children—
all blond and blue sailors—had arsenic in their bedtime milk.

It's all unnatural death.
After fires spread radiation through the air, across the ground, into
grass fed on by cows, into berries and the mushrooms she still forages,
villagers were given a place and a pension, outside the Zone.

They came back against advice. Shoot us and dig the grave, they said.
When you leave your village, you leave your soul. Replant an old tree,
    and it dies.
They pose by blue and orange embroidery—a framed piece showing
Jesus Christ with an open book that says, Love one another.

MATTHEW DICKMAN
Shooting Dogs

Do you remember when we were standing
around the park
waiting for something cool to happen
and that friend of ours
walked up to a very orange cat
and kicked it into the sky
like a soccer ball, like the exact opposite of what
the animal was, and how it
seemed to stay in the sky and never come back
down with its fur
and internal bleeding and how the skinheads
sitting on the picnic table
rushed us like a mom, like a dad,
and made a kind of soup out of our friend and you
and I just stood there watching
the trees move, the way they moved just a little,
just a little-little, like a tongue, like a jaw,
back and forth in the sky,
the fucking sky, I can't believe how the sky can be
sometimes, it just gets away with everything
beneath it no matter what,
it just moves clouds around, it just makes it rain
or not rain, it can be so boring,
it can make you do things you never thought you
could do. I guess there's power in that.
I guess things could be worse. We could be
shooting dogs, we could be shooting them in great
numbers and making a mountain
out of the leashes and collars, we could be pulling
the gold from their teeth afterwards,
or just making all the dogs walk through the streets
without any clothes on. When you're waiting
for something to happen

you are probably falling in love, probably really
wanting to take someone home
and kiss them and make them shake like a honeymoon.

Butterflies

Upside down overhead projectors from yellow grade school

We say your name and we clap for you

Our small
small bodies and our
big big heads

Eyes on everything

They look like thinking
Mud-puddling in mud
or alcohol

I lie on my back with my feet in the air

An egg stuck on a leaf a hundred eggs
A chandelier

The Auto-Tune left on in the backyard beneath the trees it just makes
    everything feel better

Take one by mouth every hour

The Lives of My Friends

The sun may be bright but it is not clear
To me why I feel as I do, feeling my way

Along the shadowy sidewalks that show
No traces of the footprints that should

Have worn the concrete down to earth,
No hard evidence of the lives of my friends

Or scrap of fabric upon a random thorn;
Their jackets, coats, and winter wraps

Boxed or tossed or sold to vintage shops
With shirts and pants and summer frocks;

Their ties and scarves and woolen hats
Gone to build the wings of moths;

They loved to let their rooms grow dark.
And when they died they gave away their hearts.

CAMILLE DUNGY

Frequently Asked Questions: 7

Is it difficult to get away from it all once you've had a child?

I am swaying in the galley—working
       to appease this infant who is not

fussing but will be fussing if I don't move—
       when a black steward enters the cramped space

       at the back of the plane. He stands by the food carts
prepping his service. Then he is holding his throat

the way we hold our throats when we think we are going to die.
I'm sorry. I'm so sorry. He is crying. *My God. What they did to us.*

I am swaying lest my brown baby girl make a nuisance
       of herself, and the steward is crying honest man tears.

       Seeing you holding your daughter like that—for the first time,
I understand what they did to us. All those women sold away

       from their babies, he whispers. I am at a loss now.
Perhaps I could fabricate an image to represent this

       agony, but the steward has walked into the galley
of history. There is nothing figurative about us.

STEPHEN DUNN
The Architect

loved the Mobius, and the sky's big suggestion
      of a universe, and now and then
would imagine a heaven as if it were his

to construct and manage, death just a pause
      before the real work would begin.
In truth, and in his practice, he preferred things

that had endings, was sure that anything
      that goes on and on
was destined to mislead, be shapeless,

false. But still the idea appealed to him
      the way feelings appeal
to those who feel they should be thinking.

Some, the innocent, would call him the architect
      of infinity, which he wouldn't correct,
while the rest of us kept as quiet as we could.

Etheridge Knight's "Feeling Fucked Up"

The Cray Revisitation

Lord she's gone done left me been confiscated / up and split up
and I with no laws to make her
come back and everywhere the handmade helms are jade
bright manifesto white   crystal disinfo glistens
Batman Gabby Giffords Sandy Hook and Charleston drove
Mz Firearms away made her take her Rights and her Amen d ments
and her purples and her floral silencers—

Fuck Heroes and tambourines and vibra-slaps drifting in the sky
fuck the Multiverse and teaching and the dome and drones
and anthologies and all the ice that surrounds our flat earth
fuck cosby and caitlyn fuck the truth community and CERN and
social engineering and intelligent design fuck viagra and Apple
and genetically modified organisms fuck the star elders
low earth A.I. and all the gang stalking fuck sandra bernie bland sanders
and black lives matter fuck the hoax whores fuck freedom reform forms fuck
the whole fatherfucking thing
all I want now is my Mama Gun back
so my soul can ammo

KIRBY GANN
The Obscening of Engine Kreuter

People called his music inspired and wicked. They said the man was gifted with crazy guitar fingers that could make you weep one moment and get you shouting *hot damn* the next. His first manager used to brag to any ear that would listen: *Take your girl to hear him, Kreuter will get you laid*—and it was true, or at least it was back in the day when he first broke into the clubs and there were aficionados eager to spread the word, to be the first in the know. Even the tone deaf could hear he had that guitar by the throat. Even the indifferent could hear his gift for creating insightful, unusual, often extraordinary songs.

He was also a noted failure. The precise phrase welcomed him as he and his wife, Nadine, entered the office of Gideon Revels for this most unlikely of meetings: *The noted failure*, Revels greeted him, gleefully, offering a broad manicured hand, a gold star embedded in the nail of his little finger. "You must be wondering how after all those years of toil you find yourself here. You two like kiwi?"

The man went to a bar that stretched along one far wall of his office before either Kreuter or his wife could answer, Revels praising the blended-juice recipe he downed daily about this time. *For physical vigor*, he said, slapping his flanks as though sizing up a horse; *for self-collection and mental energy.* He returned with two tall cylindrical glasses filled with a substance the color of a bruise, and his smile flashed teeth that appeared to have been sharpened. "I'm not even going to tell you how busy I am, you two've been around long enough to know," Revels said as he sat down behind his desk. "But here you are. Tell me something I want to hear."

Nadine spoke first. "Gideon, my husband has proven his brilliance over and over and these new songs are so expansive and true, you'll hear genius at work here, it's a new album, a totally new direction."

"It's a new direction with every album is my understanding," Revels said. "That's admirable. It's possibly the whole problem. You get so into the art you forget the audience. My man Sykes here"—with his head he indicated a young man, not much more than a boy, who had snuck in unannounced—"Sykes, he's been filling me in on your history, the bits I didn't know already. You've moved a few thousand units before. That's nice. Seems the only people who know your music are other musicians—and that's fine. Admirable. But it doesn't get you on the cover of *Spin*, does it?"

"That's why we're here," she said. "We've tried it on our own long enough."

Kreuter wasn't sure what to expect from this meeting, and yet he had earned it too—to be in such a well-appointed office, platinum albums glimmering on the walls, the skyline vista out the high-rise windows. He had sat in such offices before, years ago. Instead of Cressida Six, the most recent diva phenomenon, the albums then were by Ratt and Poison and Tom Petty. He had been hardly more than a teenager when his band's first album charted well despite being against the hair-metal fashion of the moment—a surprise success that stashed five boys into tour buses for eighteen months, time enough for them to learn to despise one another. Kreuter had provided the songs, so he hadn't worried long over the breakup, launching headfirst into the promise of a solo career that was now sixteen years old and yet to pan out.

Each of his five albums had appeared on a label smaller than the one before, three of which no longer existed. There were no more tour buses, only an Aerostar towing a rickety trailer. He was careening toward middle age and still renting an apartment over a friend's garage, still living without regular health insurance; he wasn't above giving the odd lesson or five to children of wealthy fans, these patrons who inevitably expressed their surprise at how easy it was to reach him, pleased that an equation as simple as a friend of a friend of a friend could lead to an expensive, unforgettable birthday present to a guitar-loving son or daughter.

His wife, Nadine, was doing what she could, driven to right what she called *an almost cosmic wrong*. As the talent buyer at Montreux's historic music club, Throat, she had contacts but was otherwise only human. Circumstances had driven them to go it alone some three years before, when the last album failed to earn out and Kreuter lost his label again. Then his longtime manager/friend/main creditor, Gian Kazimier—*Kaz*, the only man who called Engine by his given name, Emil Jim—died from the heart attack they had both half expected, had even joked about, would come one day due to his unrepentant love of "cocaine, amphetamines / any make to help you dream," as the line from Kreuter's "Talkin' Montreux Blues" put it.

Now Sykes moved into their line of sight. He looked as if he had just stepped from college graduation, model-handsome if too small by a foot, blond cherub curls still damp from a shower (though it was past noon) or else whorled with some kind of goop, his green eyes aglow over a tie blue-bright enough to invoke tropical lizards. "*Positioning*," he said. "That's what we're on about." Unlike Revels, when he smiled, he kept his lips closed.

"I don't want to soundtrack a car commercial," Kreuter told his wife.

"Or some ED medicine," she agreed.

Revels laughed. "We're nowhere near placing your music in either of those markets, but I like how you're thinking. So what have you got for us?"

What Kreuter had was a CD of eleven unmastered tracks cherry-picked from an album in process. The loss of Kaz had taken so much that it might as well have been everything, but over the course of his grief it also gave rise to more songs than Kreuter knew properly what to do with. He demoed thirty of them on the four-track in his bedroom. Nadine called much of it the best work he had ever done, and he trusted her implicitly; never once over their twelve years together had she shied from dismissing work she thought below his standard.

He rotated the disc in his hands while mumbling his hope that they keep in mind this was only a rough mix, unmastered and thus raw. Then his wife took over as he'd hoped she would, making the pitch by linking bands and artists to his sound. "Think Jimi Hendrix in collaboration with Miles Davis," she said. "Engine's voice sits in for the horn, they're almost the same timbre. Think power, all right? But groove too, and mood…"

Revels flashed his piranha teeth again. "Let's get a taste."

All this had been started by a phone call between two old friends. A few weeks ago Kreuter had been struggling with a set of troublesome lyrics, a task made more difficult by the hours of animated conversation Nadine was having on the kitchen line with a woman named Muriel, her close girlfriend from a happily misspent youth in New York. Kreuter had never met the woman, he'd heard only stories. He had been staring at a list of words that rhymed with *alms* when his wife said her goodbyes and gave him the relief of a quiet moment; then she accosted him, unable to contain her excitement, clawing his shoulders as she squealed her optimism and announced their next strategic move: she was going to deliver her husband in person to no one less than Gideon Revels.

Kreuter thought to check the cabinet where they stashed their stash to see what she must have imbibed. Revels was one of the golden gods, the renowned impresario behind the latest sensations of which Cressida Six served as crown: young women gyrating between purity and Sodom, busting stripper moves on air-hangar stages while lip-synching songs written by committees. What possible interest could he have in a grizzled road dog like Engine Kreuter?

"Don't be negative"—Nadine poked his chest—"we're in. There's an army at work there, all kinds of up-and-comers. What matters is he's the boss and my girlfriend's fucking him. I *know* Muriel, so don't worry, he'll listen. We'll get the minutes."

Kreuter was still earnest and idealistic about many things, but he understood how business often got done. So why not. He left the impossible to her and took control of what he could: recording. He agonized over the sale of three invaluable guitars to finance the work, saving money by playing all instruments but the drums himself, and recording at odd hours to cash in on favors owed Kaz by a solid sound engineer. The sessions soon felt like a last testament, not so much a summing up as a final chance, as if he'd pledged to commit every pressure, stress, fear, and joy from thirty-eight years of living rough to two-inch tape. Yet even as he experimented with instrumentation, the songs felt sturdy enough by the end that he could hear how to strip them down live; he would need only a couple of bandmates willing to work for scale to cover a short tour. And then, he feared—and if previous experience was anything to go by—the time would come for him to walk away. No one pays to see a middle-aged man ply his desperations on a stage. He would assume his mantle of notable failure and search out a stable method for making a living.

He was at the studio when Nadine called. The news she dropped set his belly to a boil, thrust him into a state of panicked disbelief that only increased over the long drive to New York (Kreuter avoided flying whenever possible): They had twenty minutes with the man himself.

"She must be something else in bed, your girlfriend," he whispered in wonder.

"They don't make it to bed, that's the key, hon," his wife said, lamenting as she often did how little her husband understood of the world.

As they listened, Kreuter fought the urge to explain his intentions with each song as it arose, where it succeeded and where it struggled and how it could be improved; he fought the urge to question the surprisingly crude boom box Revels kept in his office for listening. Instead he allowed himself to admire the surprises and curiosities he'd suffered to inscribe in his songs. The music modified itself over time, songs as shape-shifters, guitar vamps morphing to jazz chord voicings, six-string acoustics melding into twelve-string electric and then into cello and then piano and even, in one particularly inspired instance, kazoo. He took it as a positive that the album was nearing its full forty-eight minutes and there they were still, listening. As the last track began, when he realized they were going to roll through the entire album without a word, he was almost happy.

"That is…well, now," said the boy Sykes in a near-whisper, seemingly hesitant to break the silence that followed.

"Nice," Revels added. His voice sounded like something with all the juice squeezed out of it. "I like it."

Nadine squeezed Kreuter's thigh just above the knee.

"Only—you know what? It's missing one crucial sound."

"You must be high," Nadine said. "Nothing's missing, that was magic. That sounded better than anything I've heard on the radio in years."

"What you hear on the radio is money," Revels said. "My ears, they cut through the art and hear the money. Not knocking your work, I get it, this is good, your stuff makes me want to go daydream at home and, I don't know, contemplate my Rothkos."

"We can always remix," Nadine suggested then, reclaiming her hand from Kreuter's leg. "You've got a guy, I'm sure." Revels' predacious smile flashed again; he complimented her on the clean sharpness of her mind.

"*Listen*," Nadine said. She told him of how she expected to leave today with a clear path moving forward, to at least *start* to put the world right in regard to her husband's work, so of course they were open to Revels' established guidance. Who did he have in mind?

Revels shrugged, asked, "Who else would I use?"

He tapped the same technician anytime he needed to launch an artist—*or save one:* Pim (just Pim), London's producer-genius of the day, renowned for his hand behind a staggering number of Top Ten singles. Kreuter recognized his work everywhere, which mined oblique samples from Great American Songbook tunes, fattened percussion to rival the drums, and usually added some kind of shock ambient noise. He'd thought it fun and interesting the first few hundred times he'd heard it. Applied to his own endeavor, however, the only end-product he could imagine was absurd. But then again the past twenty years proved how much Kreuter lacked the popular touch.

"So long as my husband gets final approval," Nadine said. She had her tough voice out now, not interested in reassurances, telling it like it is. A trait of hers he loved so long as the voice wasn't directed at him.

"The music's there," Sykes said as he moved from where he had been standing out of view. "We get Pim on board, that whole area takes care of itself. The music's the least of our worries."

"See how good this kid is? Knows exactly when to drop the bomb," pronounced Revels proudly. "You can't teach this stuff."

"The bomb?" Kreuter and his wife asked together.

"Always a bomb to drop when talking business."

"First," Sykes began, "know that I'm a fan. Still, when Gideon dropped this particular bomb on me—your career—I went back and studied your albums more closely. I wouldn't say it's *an acquired taste*, but you demand repeated listenings. It holds up under repeated listening too, I might add, but that doesn't tell me why you've remained so, if you'll forgive me the word, *obscure*."

"I've always assumed tough luck. Not getting heard by the right people at the right time," Kreuter got in.

"Positioning?" Nadine offered, to the boy's accelerating nods.

"To do this we need to get to work," Sykes said. "We have to remake your profile, fast. You're too old to be hopped out as the best new thing. What we'll do is show listeners you've been here all along, only stepping out to them now."

Gideon interrupted, unable to cede the stage any longer: "Music isn't all that starts people talking about musicians. You know this. We got acts with albums dropping soon, we get them to reference Engine Kreuter as an influence, yeah? Maybe you lay down guitar on somebody recording right now, Sykes, we haven't wrapped Cressida's new one yet have we? By the time our little boutique label releases your album, suddenly you're this underground grandpa-boy of rock. Bridging the generations, dropping hard-earned wisdom on the youngsters. Strikes a vibe to your name, maybe pulls you past that core audience you've built through van-and-trailer tours."

Engine stroked the stripe of gray astride his chin, the most obvious sign of his rock-elder status. He would shave. "I would love to retire that van," he admitted.

"Once our mutual friend Muriel laid this job on me—best thing to ever happen for you, let me say up front—well, we started digging around to see what anyone thought of Engine Krueter. Sykes, tell us what you found out."

"Nicest guy in the business."

"*A rather earnest fellow*," sneered Revels. "Kreuter writes thank-you notes to the clubs he plays. *Handmade*. Kreuter renegotiates the guarantee if shows don't make their expected audience. That is not rock 'n' roll. You know it's not."

"It's true, Emil," Nadine said, "you've been shit on as long as I've known you. I love the kind man I married but you're too nice out there in the world."

"You're a toilet, an outhouse," Revels added helpfully. "You're the flush after I've taken a big dump—"

"OK OK I get it," Kreuter said.

The combined gazes of Revels and his protégé were upon him, examining him, he supposed, to see how he held up. He decided his best move would be to call the end of the meeting himself, rather than being told to go. "One last thing," he said.

It was a difficult question to get out; he didn't know how to phrase it, how to assert a sliver of dignity here, with him and Nadine essentially peasants seeking favor from their king. "Why are you doing this? This is way beyond a favor for your lady."

"Believe me, I'm doing no favors; this is business." Revels' grin grew tight and his bald skull reddened. "Look, you want honesty? I'm all honesty with my clients. The market has proved me a man who can do no wrong; everything I've touched over the past decade has turned to gold. No, platinum. I am content, see. And that's dangerous." His face relaxed and he swept a palm over the length of it. "The kind of money

I make, the tax bracket I'm in? Let's just say it would not suck if I took a loss this year or next, son."

Son? Kreuter thought—Revels was easily five years his junior.

"Well, I thank you for your time, and appreciate your willingness to take a chance on me. I'll do my best not to disappoint—"

Revels slapped away his extended hand with the back of his own.

"That's exactly what we've been talking about, Kreuter, cut that shit out! Don't thank me or Sykes here till we've all made money. From now on, whenever, wherever you show up, you let everybody know *you don't need to be there.* Understand? You're just doing a favor for someone else."

It was either a new beginning or the final defeat.

Somehow Revels booked Kreuter on the second stage at the Sussex Music Festival, one of the biggest summer events in the UK. From there he would embark on a twelve-date tour supporting some ska band he'd never heard of but who he understood enjoyed a fervent following. His new album would drop the day he arrived. Already this was large-scale career progress, a feat he and Nadine would never have finagled on their own. He rounded out a band with two musicians willing to work cheap: Frank Worley, the drummer on the album, reliably familiar and almost a friend despite the decade between their ages, and Knox Reusnach, aka *Knock-Knock,* practically a kid but Sykes had recommended him and he'd impressed at his audition, a scrawny talent equally comfortable on bass, guitar, and keys who knew his way around a Moog. The lean setup encouraged a simpler sound—good for introducing music to listeners live—and in rehearsals they found the simplicity left room for more expansive play. Music started to surprise him again; on the way to another rehearsal, Kreuter realized, unexpectedly, an honest relish at doing a tour with these two in a foreign land.

Still, the anxieties: he had yet to hear the final mix of the album. He had given himself up to it and doubted the decision every few minutes of every day. Four months had passed since the meeting, over which time Pim sent samples via Sykes. Kreuter had bristled at what he heard: his natural sound retreating before Pim's slick sheen, every beat cranked up to a shuddering thump. He would've pulled out if not for his poverty, his lack of other options, and Nadine. She was his calmative, reminding him now was the time for compromise, he had had years of doing it his way.

"Besides," she said, massaging his temples while his head lay in her lap, "I like what I hear."

"You find a set of Revels' ears to put on?" He kept his eyes closed to the headache she knew how to rub away.

Nadine chuckled, her breath sweetened by the joint they shared. "Maybe yeah. Maybe I hear some money here." She tapped in time with toms the producer had added in. "Ease up on the ideals, baby, you're in good hands." And in the moments following, as her fingers plowed over his scalp and beneath his jaw, he believed he was.

He scribbled notes and sent them on and tried to feel reassured by the glad-handing responses that came back—Pim *loved* his ideas, as if that clarified anything. He told himself the man wasn't intent on desecrating his compositions, there was reverence for another's work among musicians. Such self-coaching, along with Ambien and benzodiazepines, kept him steady.

As the day of departure crept closer, discussions with his wife turned less on music and more toward the scope of medications he would require. To overcome his panic attacks and general anxiety; to lift his spirits when sleepless travel exhausted his body, or drop him into dreams when performance addled him.

"Sykes says he's got a guy in London," she said.

"Getting to London is what worries me." Flying terrified him. Again Nadine assured him she had Sykes taking care. Before he left, Kreuter kissed her like he feared he would never see her again, like he was embarking on a journey as dramatic and irrevocable as a soldier called off to war. "I'd have better hold of all this if you were traveling with me," he said. She'd refused to go, claiming the club needed her home.

She scrubbed the thorny crown that passed for his hair. "Remember, we asked for this. I'll be here when you get back. All you have to do is get out there and play like only Engine Kreuter can. Find us some friends."

Friends being her slang for cash bills in hand.

The band caught its connecting flight at La Guardia. There they arrived without fanfare and slipped into the buzz of the scene, where it seemed everyone scurried about in preparation for the Sussex festival. Revels' company had booked a number of their acts to the same flight, though Revels himself was already in London, leaving Sykes to square Kreuter and his bandmates. The boy came through as promised too, slipping Kreuter a melange of pharmaceuticals in the travelers lounge with instructions to take two blue pills and wait an hour to see how his body reacted before taking any more. Kreuter downed three immediately in front of him as a display of independence. An hour later, once he took his seat in the row behind the open curtains allowing view of the good life in the first-class cabin, he downed two more. Sykes sat up there, somewhere. Cressida Six and her entourage were supposed to be up there as well, but he had yet to spot her.

He both did and did not care if he saw her. He didn't because celebrity meant nothing to him, and yet a part of him wondered if the singer even knew who he was or that they had ostensibly "worked together"—not long after that initial meeting Revels had astonished him by arranging for Kreuter to provide guitar on one of her singles. Some fluff about sexing the night. The easiest money he'd ever made, adding soundscape color for the most part, except for nine bars in the middle and six toward the end, the signature the simplest 4/4. He'd been in the studio no more than a few hours and never laid eyes on the singer herself.

He was about to slip on his headphones when a bustle up front distracted him as more passengers straggled in, late—the flight was already ten minutes past the scheduled departure time. The plane shuddered beneath bumping luggage and the overhead compartments banging shut, a reminder of the structure's fragility that made him queasy. And then there she was, his eye drawn automatically to a wild pompom of cotton-candy blue hair shaking over a set of bare and shapely shoulders and the trill of her fingers as she acknowledged her audience of gawking passengers. A gesture mastered by royalty and pageant queens that she performed, he could tell, without a thought. Cressida Six, "rhymes with *peace*," as she liked to repeat (repeated ad nauseam in one of her inescapable summer hits). Kreuter was so struck by how small and lovely she was in real life that a moment passed before his animosity returned—the girl and her ilk stood for all that estranged him. He held a theory that her kind of music went hand in hand with the dumbing down of the entire culture, the twilight dimming of thought. Still, he had taken her money for a job. He didn't care how many levels of hypocrite this made of him. He resented her for that, too.

Fortunately, he had the headphones and CD player to distract him, along with the second gift Sykes had provided: a copy of the finished album. (Sykes understood Kreuter would refuse listening to the poorer quality compression of an mp3; Kreuter respected the kid for that measure of thoughtfulness.) He pressed *play* and then *pause* once the attendants launched into the preflight routine he'd always viewed as false hope to the doomed but felt obligated to follow anyway. He slipped two more blues into his mouth as the plane taxied onto the runway, rolling the pills on his tongue, cradling them between his teeth, unable to swallow until they were aloft and the landing gear was up and he was amazed yet again that they weren't all dead.

He worried the pills were duds. So far, he felt little more than a soft tone spreading through his limbs, as though his cells had begun to exchange pleasantries, along with a cushioning in the flesh around his eyes. What he wanted was a sedative's seductive pull from below, to help him listen to his own album with open ears.

He couldn't put this off any longer, and pressed *play* again.

Instantly the changes were apparent. They had rearranged the order of songs, opening with the track he had planned as the closer. They had modified its beginning as well, adding a cold, dreamy piano that drifted slow high notes transposed from the bass line that took over the song's final third. Pim's burnished sheen gave the sound a big-room feel, overamplifying what he had intended to be intimate. It sounded like radio. Still it was what he had expected, and he supposed he could live with it. Was this the sound of money? He had no idea. He had no choice but to accept it anyway. As of tomorrow the album belonged to the world, no longer his.

The second song began so strangely that he rechecked the screen to see if the disc was actually a mix of different artists and not solely his own work. A voice not his own counted down to an unfamiliar drum track, a new four-on-the-floor beat that catapulted the song close to a disco jam, and Kreuter's ears balked.

He begged the passing attendant for a cabernet. She must have sensed his desperation, as she delivered one promptly. He sucked it down as alarm took hold through the third track, into the fourth...he recognized the songs as those he had written, but they were nothing like the songs he had made. The producer had manipulated his sound to such a degree that, in growing despair, he half expected to hear Cressida Six with her synthetic sighs instead of his own voice. He'd been stripped from his own music, forced into prefab molds for nineteen-year-olds dropping X. Halfway through the album, he knew he wouldn't make it to the end. His speeding heart throbbed in his chest and into his shoulders. He yanked the earphones from his head and stood up, hands clenched, ready to hurl the player hard through the curtains and into first class, smacking Sykes or that ridiculous singer on the head. It was only Worley from the row behind asking if he was all right that brought him to his senses. Kreuter's skin felt incendiary, his palms sweating, a trickle running down the small of his back; he didn't answer because he couldn't, he could merely look at his bandmate a moment before sitting down again.

He was a grown-up, an artist, a professional. His career a disaster. He felt hollowed and angry and strange. His breathing seemed off. He thought he might claw through the window. He demanded another wine and ignored the glass, drained the bottle in one swift swallow. For fuck's sake, he kept thinking. For fuck's sake, what had he given himself to? And then the pills kicked in and the undertow arrived, strong in a great wave that pulled him down and under. He welcomed the plunge; he dove deep.

In the holding cell beneath Heathrow airport—a windowless cement room not unlike the green rooms he recalled from the few stadium shows played so long ago, in the early days—Kreuter stared at the zip ties binding his wrists while he listened to his bandmates describe the violence of a madman who had erupted on the flight while he slept. Only the ties, the police outside the door, and his immediate surroundings could convince him that they were not making up a story as part of an elaborate prank. In the dullness of his aching brain he sought to account for the man they described.

"Really, you remember none of this?" asked Revels through his big smile, his sharp teeth on permanent display. Sykes was nowhere to be seen.

"You probably don't remember stabbing me, then," Knock-Knock said, fiddling with a bandage over his palm and flexing his hand experimentally. He held up the hand to show a grisly little wound to the meat of his thumb. "You were something else, boss. A real maniac. Like Jack the Ripper crazy. Gave everybody a flight to remember, I'll tell you that."

"I stabbed you?"

"I guess I was kind of asking for it. But you weren't about to get off Cressida Six on your own."

The wound wasn't the only evidence. In the plane after he awoke, and after the marshal freed him from where he had been strapped into his seat, two officers helped Kreuter to his feet and up the aisle. Near the front row of first class they'd paused briefly beside a contained scene of debauchery: bits of food clung to the walls, and what looked like an explosion of paste lay drying in white scabs and splotches, a smear bisecting one window. The air there smelled sickly sweet—the stench like the morning after an all-night party—and a long burgundy stain arced from the wall above and across the magazine pockets and onto the floor, ending where an array of cutlery lay scattered. The sight struck a dark, dismaying chord within him; Kreuter knew, somehow, the mess was his.

The chord deepened and expanded as he listened to Worley and Knock-Knock recount a story almost impossible to believe. But only *almost*—throughout the frustrating years he'd sought to deny the embittered, raging man he seemed to helplessly watch being born within him, layer atop layer of each successive disappointment, the silent indifference that greeted each new failure at odds with the glamorous triumph of every undeserving other. Or maybe they had been deserving, it didn't matter; he knew only that there seemed to be no room for him. Despite his certainty that his art was all he was there to do.

At points the tale felt vaguely familiar, as though repeating events from a movie seen long ago and forgotten until now, a story that kept Revels queerly entertained and beaming. Kreuter had awakened from a nap and asked for something to drink; the stewardess was involved in other duties at the time and told him he'd have to wait; the wait proved to be too long, and he stood tall to make an announcement to his fellow passengers: he would serve himself. The path to the galley was blocked by a food cart without any wine on it, so he snatched a bottle of water and then proceeded to climb over the seats to get around the cart. This set off complaints that Kreuter shushed, as though he could manage his journey without anyone's notice, until someone pushed him off into the aisle and he fell. When he got back up, he poured the water over the steward who'd come to help. "They kept telling you to return to your seat, but you weren't having none of that," Knock-Knock said.

"You said you could see how busy they all were and you could support yourself, thank you very much, you used to be a bartender. Is that true? You used to tend bar?"

"No," Kreuter said. "Never." He closed his eyes. Knock-Knock laughed.

They gave him the wine and led him back to his seat, and he was calmed for the better part of an hour. The next time he got up, however, he pushed through the curtains into first class. "Hello people! It's Engine Kreuter—the genius artist you've never heard of. Now's your chance: get to know me!" Nobody took him up on the offer. He spotted an empty seat beside Cressida Six and sat down beside her. At first, they chatted amicably. Worley said he had no idea about what, and Revels said he'd kill to know, he wondered if "Cress" would tell him…But then things turned strange. This was a moment they hoped Kreuter might remember: what happened with the young singer. Witnesses said their conversation grew heated, and soon the two were arguing outright. Kreuter began to insult her music—loudly, and inviting other passengers to join in and agree— proclaiming that surely she wasn't so dim as to think her music was what brought fans to her shows. She was all about liberating her sexy self, wasn't she? Why not perform *that*? If she were truly the artist she blathered on about being in interviews, Kreuter couldn't understand why she kept to the pretension of playing a concert. Her concerts were a mask, she wasn't liberating anyone from anything but their money. She should just let a soundtrack roll—it was already anyway, with her prerecorded vocals—and do a striptease or whatever. Or better yet, *have sex onstage*, as that's what everyone wanted from her. Plant a guy in the audience (or even a girl!) and pretend they've been chosen for the task…He said he would be glad to partner her, he was a teacher at heart. And then Kreuter reached for her.

The empty seat belonged to her bodyguard, who had been in the toilet when Kreuter stumbled up. Said bodyguard returned the moment Kreuter embraced her, and the first-class cabin became a combat zone.

"You rammed him with the cart and upended the thing," Worley told him. "We were trying to calm you down, one of the pilots had come out too. You threw a tub of yogurt and grabbed a fork off the floor and started swiping at everyone—the bodyguard, the pilot, me, but Knock-Knock's the one you hit."

From beneath a headlock, Kreuter had insisted *You just don't know who I am. Nobody here knows me. Nobody here knows my fucking name.* The spectacle ended quickly once he slipped free and turned to the emergency door, announcing he'd had enough, he was leaving. "How in hell do you get out of this place?" he shouted. He got a hand onto the long red bar that unlocked the door and three of them—the pilot, the bodyguard, and Knock-Knock—took him to the floor.

"It was pretty extraordinary," Knock-Knock said. "Man, you were a real menace to society. I never would've guessed you had that in you."

Kreuter worried he had that and more inside him. A strong urge to curl up on the concrete bench and wrap his arms about his head, to fold into that position taught during disaster drills at elementary school, took hold. He emptied the liter of water Revels had given him and then covered his eyes, wallowing in his ruin. "I'm so sorry, guys," he said finally.

"We're good," Knock-Knock replied. "It was punk rock."

"Brought you all this way for no reason. I've wasted your time."

Revels' grand smile broadened into a gleeful laugh as he stood up, clapping Kreuter on the shoulders before pulling him into a great bear hug. "Are you insane, Engine? Get a load of this guy, boys! Best thing to happen to him in twenty years and he thinks he's ruined us all!" He released Kreuter from his grip and started to pace wall to wall. "You've got charges, yeah, we're not sure what yet, we can assume public intoxication and maybe assault, I don't know what the airline will say about damage to the cart and carpet. But this is no pay-your-fine-and-go deal. We'll get a trial. That'll be another year probably, right? A year with your name out there. We'll milk this as long as we can. Don't worry about Cress, she's a pro, I'll smooth it. We're here to find out your bond, that's all, and then we're off. The show goes on, mate."

"What were those pills you gave me?"

"Honestly don't know. Hey, I didn't make this happen. Or hell, maybe I did. I'm about to start believing those pills were magic. Son, you are now a bona fide *rock star.*"

As in all things marketable, Revels was right. Kreuter stepped outside the airport into a world that wanted to speak with him, to find out who he was and what he had to say. There were interviews. The English weeklies proclaimed Engine Kreuter "the pure American soul of rock 'n' roll." At Sussex he shredded the stage. He made a cameo during Cressida Six's set that showcased what he could do with that guitar. When the song ended, she received an awesome roar of approval after telling the audience that, had they been somewhere more private, she might've let the old man teach her a thing or two, after all.

Revels pulled him from the ska-band tour after three dates so that Kreuter could headline his own. His band worked to revise their sound to better reflect the formula Pim had created. Whatever doubts Kreuter still held against such changes dissipated under the immutable velocity of it all.

Now he's working on what comes next; his new contract requires an album in the can by spring. He feels he knows what he's doing and it all comes easier than before. His sound comes closer to what he hears on the radio, and though he feels it has lost the singular edge that once gave him such pride, he has larger concerns these days, other people's income now reliant on him.

He jokes with Nadine that he owes his new life to five hours of which he has no memory. Sometimes, at odd moments, usually just as he falls asleep, slippery details return: certain colors of light, the vibrations in the floor beneath his feet, the smell of wine. He can almost remember Cressida Six on that airplane, almost recall how he had touched her. There had been a strangeness to her breast, an unfamiliar perfection; it had been so full, so firm, so—manufactured. It was like nothing he had ever touched before, and he remembers it as promise, as beautiful, as something of which he would never ever let go.

Self-Portrait As Mango

She says, *Your English is great! How long have you been in our country?*
I say, *Suck on a mango, bitch, since that's all you think I eat anyway.* Mangoes

are what model minorities like me know nothing about, right? Doesn't
a mango just win spelling bees and kiss white boys? Isn't a mango

a placeholder in a poem folded with saris? But this one, the one
I'm going to shove down her throat, is a mango

that remembers jungles jagged with insects, the river's darker thirst.
This mango was cut down by a scythe that beheaded soldiers, a mango

that taunts and suns itself into a hard-palmed fist only a few months
a year, fattens while blood stains green ponds. Why use a mango

to beat her to death? Why not a coconut? Because this "exotic" fruit
won't be cracked open to reveal its own whiteness to you. This mango

isn't alien merely because of a bone-hard brown shell. I know
I'm worth waiting for, I want to be kneaded for ripeness. Mango:

my own sunset-skinned heart waiting to be held and peeled, mango
Ammu taught me to cut open with teeth. *This, Tarfia, is how you eat a mango.*

JERZY FICOWSKI
Apocrypha of the Original Apple

Translated by Jennifer Grotz and Piotr Sommer

Verily it is the Apple
that wants to be eaten
Apple of sweet ignorance
of good and evil
a dappled, appley, appleton
squeezed inside itself
like a fist
reeling until hurt by its own seeds

Around its own impatience
it quickly revolves to eve
so that she might have
all the blushing all at once

And sayeth the Apple
verily I am the Apple
that wants to be eaten
to know your tongue
your teeth the roof of your mouth
Taste me let it be
as moses commanded

However eve devours beneath her eyelids
the Sight of the Apple
and by winking divides
its nourishing blushes
into bites
she doesn't even touch the Apple

filled to the tips of her lashes
by its red cry

And the Apple insane
flies off the branch
And eve falls
under the apple's blow

ANNE-MARIE FYFE
Blue Skies, Nothing But Blue Skies

Sidewalk vendors look askance when I ask
Am I headed East or West? I could
tell them I navigate by the sky's color
but it wrong-foots me time and again.
What sky? they say, looking up. The one
that cracked wide one bright September,
while we were looking away, the one
that enchanted Portuguese cartographers,
the sky that sheltered a century's huddles,
a parasol over sidewalks, wharves, fire trucks,
ferry boats, and strings of bulbs on lighted bridges,
over sixteen miles of serene Canaletto clouds.
No, not any of those… And yet
all of them. And my pale blue heaven too,
that I watched from childhood's promontories
on an ocean's edge, miles from the here and now.

ROSS GAY
Blowjob

It's just like the tongue, isn't it,
to fold you up
into a tiny origami swan
whose angled wings
splay and whose jutted neck
and beak point out over some expanse
of water a tugboat
hauling the mammoth frigate
upstream the reckless kayaker
tickling an eddy
the currents changing temperature
beneath your feet
as you paddle nowhere except into
the mouth of the one who
made you

DAVID GEWANTER
Wellfleet, Off-Season

The walls inside the city buildings curve, glass and plaster bending in thigh-shape, or breast-shape, a comfort to patients in RECEPTION, waiting to have their griefs or gallbladders removed, tumors and proud flesh pulled from the body, snipped off by the healer

who has no sodden breast to offer in return, no nutriment, but only a body that seeks and sops up the danger. When our pustule is punctured, drained of its milk,

what relief! Like a curse forgiven, or clean baby lifted from the tub; purgation dribbling onto the Greek tiles of theater, the puddle of mother's blood, the son's eyeballs rolling. All this, gulped by the doctors…

The analysts swallow the story hour, listening to terrors, lies, and self-stroking flattery until, with small polite coughs, they clear the pulp from their throats. Next hour, they will swallow fire—

Rheum, rickets, rabbit fever; raccoon eyes; shrinking or bloating, drooping, spilling—Our briny sorrows, our growths and killing sugars flow toward doctors daily, drying into a gray dust of pity, caking their skin, glutting the ears…

At night, they drive the glistening streets, circling round the old monuments that pinch and strangle the homeward traffic, like stone ghosts of parents blocking a new idea…two more months, is it? or two weeks, or tomorrow, and they will come

to Wellfleet, and fill the bayside beach in ranks of beach chairs, attending the ceremony of waves, the dithering water that rises and topples over, then gathers its resolve to stand and lunge again. One wave seems a horsetail, the next, a mother's hair…

The doctors do not read the sea, or the grindstone beach; swaddled in holiday hats and sunglasses, they doze like ancient directors on the set, while salt air and neap tide winds gently abrade the flesh, until their ash of illness crumbles and

drifts away, miseries given back to nature each August—motes for the crab to pick, mulch for the beach-flower—until, scrubbed clean, the aged ozone-babies return to their cities, ready for another year.

Now, in November, the beach performs for no one, a soup of rock and water waiting for August, washing itself absently—

Exhalations rise through cold air; clouds twist like rags, like lancets or gauze. No heroic gestures. Just headless statues of mist, darkening as their bellies grow.

REGINALD GIBBONS
Canasta

Houston, 1953

Masses of one un-housed
household added to another, all abandoned and made
to abandon their names. A non-colonnade
of gray clods. A un-quadrangle
of neo-rational obliteration. An arcade
of ashes. Ditch-buried
hordes of kin left akimbo, an imprisoned
necropolis on the verge of the vast acres of the settled
precincts of our planet—or maybe at the edge of the salted field
of remembrance, only one little creaking shed.
And in the low gray corner of the shed, a weak tangle
of the last echoes of a last word
that ever was uttered to a beloved child,
or of that child's reply. "I know how to play," I said

to my grandmother, I lied—
so wanting to be included, and interrupting her card
game in America—the card-table, the discard,
the talk in their languages, the tea—no more than a decade
after after all that hate-whipped
grief without a shroud.
Her three card-playing women friends, as displaced
as she, did not (I remember this) like to be interrupted.

It might be too much for me to say I understand
that what they did,
their canasta and bridge, their mahjong, they did
so as, even then, not to be destroyed.
And they went out together, too—converged
with fellow Theosophists and singers and even tramped
off in pants to a mossy, snakey wood
to see a migrating bird.

If, as I stood near the card-game, my grandmother reached
and touched my head—
I'm saying: if she did, I don't remember that she did.

Her own youngest son had gone all the way back there to be killed
in that war. If touch me she did,
it might have been because I, her blood-
descendant but knowing nothing—could
not have restored
to her for one second—
even if unwittingly I could
have touched her with the grace of a small child—
I could not have restored
"one iota," as she used to say, of the world
that had been obliterated, world
she never once mentioned.

DOREEN GILDROY
The Day with Both of Them

By the window
in the fancy hotel—
looking out, looking out with them.

A little coffee. A little cake.

These things have come for me.

And not a secret, but apparent
from which I come out of

how I could
stand back, and let happen

the birds, and the sea,
and the sky.

I woke up this morning
and I saw the light—

and I thought—I like living here
in the crystal gray

and I understood I would never
be the same.

What passes through me
gains a residence

as if I were some small vibrating figure:
the creatures seem vivid to me,
burnished in flame.

MARK HALLIDAY
Vanilla Cupcake Complaint

I am a vanilla cupcake
and I've come to tell you exactly how I feel.
When a vanilla cupcake speaks
you ought to show respect for its appeal,
and wonder what this cupcake will reveal.
Anxious and puzzled, basically, is how I feel.

Anxious about getting sick and getting old,
and then dying. Also quite anxious
about satisfying some desires before I get sick or old and die.
I want to be an extremely happy vanilla cupcake!

The world interferes with my wishes
and this interference puzzles me. Circumstances often develop
in which I am not glowing with joy
and that in *itself* is self-evidently puzzling—because, I mean,
I am a vanilla cupcake! I am golden yellow, I am fluffy,
I smell fresh and unambiguously sweet,
I came warm from the oven not all that long ago—
to me it feels like just a week before yesterday—
what would be the reason to frustrate me?
If someone must be frustrated, it should not be a vanilla cupcake.
My life should be the central thing providing a standard of fulfillment
against which the various frustrations of other baked goods could be
    measured.

Instead, the world besmirches and becrumbs me with frustrations
as if I were not a fresh cupcake but some scrap of burned toast
or a stale pretzel! For example,
there is no way for me to share frosting with an ongoing series of fresh
    cookies,
one per week let's say, while also being comfortably nestled beside
my sweet partner cupcake. The entire bakery is geared to prevent it.

This is annoying, and deeply puzzling, and ultimately sad.
What I feel is, if the world was going to select me to be
such a round beautiful puffed vanilla cupcake
then the world self-evidently should guarantee
the satisfying fulfillment implicit in vanilla cupcakeness per se!

My consolation in all this—limited, but nice—is
that I know how to tell you exactly how I feel
and you (out of respect for my vanilla voice) must surely feel
you have to listen.

SARAH HARWELL
Super Moon

The third one of the year it rose all over
so close it smelled the fried oil of our dinners—
its very nearness altered what we knew
as it called to us in waves of no-sound,
thinking its no-think, about circles.
After it rose from super into moon,
two smaller moons signaled from each car,
signaling assent, signaling to the moon
an acquiescence—to what,
we didn't know, as we idled on roads,
in parking lots, feeling a no-thing rise
in our throats, feeling the lights' slow circles
hinge the what above
to the what below.

ROBERT HASS
First Poem

In the dream he was a hawk with blood on its beak.
In the dream he was a hawk.

In the dream he was a woman, naked, indolent from pleasure, a gleam
   of sperm on her vaginal lips.
In the dream he was a woman.

(He could both be the woman and see the viscid fluid in the dream.)

In the dream he was a turquoise bird fashioned from blue stone by a people
   who dug it from the earth and believed it was the sky of a foreworld.
In the dream he was the turquoise bird.

In the dream his feet hurt, there was a long way still to go, lizards
   scuttling in the dust.
In the dream his feet hurt.

In the dream he was an old man, his woman gone, who woke early
   each day and made his pot of coffee and sliced bits of melons for the
   lizards and set them on the hard ground by the garden wall.
In the dream he was the old man.

The calm mouths of the lizards as they waited, themselves the color of
   the dust, meant that every creature was solitary on the earth.

In the dream the woman in the elevator took out her eye.
It was a moon in the dream.

In the dream there was a knock on the door and it was the troop of
   begging children and he said to them in mock outrage, "You! Scoot!
   This is not your day. Tuesday is your day" and the children laughed
   with great good humor.
Their day was Tuesday in the dream.

BROOKS HAXTON
The Arctic Vortex at Snooks Pond, 2014

An old man walked out onto the pond, not thinking,
while the thick ice chirped under his feet like sonar.
Clouds in the west kept scattering, so that a few stars
shone before daybreak. Paler clouds in the east
frayed at the blue edge of the planet's shadow.
The warmest groundwater seeping into the marsh
before it froze for the first time smoked, and ice flowers
formed in the smoke. Ice petals radiated from low twigs.
Ice feathers hung from the willow trunk reflected.
Spurs took shape on the black sheen just now frozen.
Farther out on the pond in the deep snow
powder sifted into cracks where the old ice
was contracting. Cracks in the snow gaped, wide
as the old man's knuckle, crisscross, so that the pond
was a white mosaic, each tile big as a dance floor.
Tracks from a fox, and from deer and rabbits, marked
the dance steps. The man at the sight of the cracked ice,
though he knew better, felt as if he might fall through.
But the clear ice under the cracks held. It was like him.

SEAMUS HEANEY
Banks of a Canal

Gustave Caillebotte, c. 1872

Say "canal" and there's that final vowel
Towing silence with it, slowing time
To a walking pace, a path, a whitewashed gleam
Of dwellings at the skyline. World stands still.
The stunted concrete mocks the classical.
Water says, "My place here is in dream,
In quiet good standing. Like a sleeping stream,
Come rain or sullen shine I'm peaceable."
Stretched to the horizon, placid ploughland,
The sky not truly bright or overcast:
I know that clay, the damp and dirt of it,
The coolth along the bank, the grassy zest
Of verges, the path not narrow but still straight
Where soul could mind itself or stray beyond.

JOHN KLEINER

Social Eros and the Methods of the Baroque

I'm surviving, Walter said.

There was sun and those small birds that Rome is full of in March. There were daisies coming up in the grass and a line of olives and Walter Meltort, the art historian, was on the phone to New York.

We've finished the morning round of papers. We've had lunch. Now we're going back into conference. Walter's voice was raspy, a little frail, like Walter himself. He had spent nearly forty years talking, writing, teaching about art—first the art of the baroque, specifically Bernini and Pastore, then Futurism. Back in Brooklyn, his wife wanted to know how Walter was feeling.

Robert called, she added. Apparently, you didn't tell him you were going.

I'm sure I did, Walter said, though actually he wasn't. I know I did.

They had been in Rome together when they were young and Robert was just a baby. They had walked in the gardens beyond the walls, pushed the carriage into gloomy churches and made love on the roof of their apartment as the streets roared with the joy of Roma victory and imagined all the shouting and horn blowing was for them. They had been happy and they had fought—some about Robert, some about the marriage, and some about art. Florence was still a painter then, still thinking of herself as one. When people would ask what she did, she'd say, I'm an artist. Or at least I make art. I mean I paint. I do pictures of things.

Those things were hard to describe. The borders unclear, the colors sometimes subtle and—to Walter at least—sometimes painfully beautiful. He thought Florence beautiful, standing at her canvas, staring deeply into it, or, probably, he should say, onto it. It was only a surface after all. Holding a brush, or taking a knife to a canvas, she was to him heroic, if only because she looked so self-forgetful. This is what Walter believed art required—a giving of yourself that amounted to obliteration.

He had once said this to Florence in a moment of tenderness and she turned on him fiercely: What do you know about art?

Walter had been back and forth to Rome over the years, always for work but never for it entirely. His first book was on the Raimondi chapel, and for three months running he had visited it every day, to see it, to measure it, to feel it. At a certain point, he was so deep in his studies he would have said the chapel was his own, though he couldn't have said exactly what that meant—that his mind designed it or his body lay in it.

The official reason this time around was *Rome Revisited—Rethinking Narratives in the Arts.* Walter had wanted Florence to come along. They could, he offered, stay on after the conference or stop off in Paris on the way or continue on to Crete—whatever she felt like doing. It might be their last chance to return there together. It would, he said, be like going home.

The conference was held in a villa at the edge of the city. Built with Carnegie money on top of an ancient aqueduct, it was by Roman standards relatively new. In the walls of its arcades were bits and pieces of marble—inscriptions mostly—that had turned up in the excavations. They took coffee in a room that contained a tiny model of the complex, as well as a giant pool table. Behind the main building were the gardens with their silvery trees and a long fountain in the shape of an idealized river. At the opening cocktail party, one of his colleagues said, gesturing with a drink in hand, "This, this is beyond privilege."

Mostly they were younger scholars whose work Walter knew only slightly or not at all. Walter had been told he could talk about anything and had decided to talk about rape. This had been an interest of his from the beginning. Or even before the beginning. Rape might, in a manner of speaking, be said to have made him an art historian, to have carried him away. He could still recall the moment it had happened, could remember the feeling of it. Sam Edgerton was lecturing on the baroque in Lawrence Hall, and as he held forth about Bernini's facility with stone, his compositional excesses, his idiosyncratic approach to movement, he flashed a slide of the *Rape of Proserpina.* Later that evening in the library, Walter pulled out Wittkower's *Bernini* and pored over the plates. The single marble tear on the girl's cheek, the god's hand sinking into her flesh, the legs twisting backward, the hair streaming, the hand raised in desperation.

It was not as though Walter were completely an innocent. He understood even then that countenancing cruelty and contemplating a representation of it were not the same thing, but he also understood that for him, the eighteen-year-old Walter Meltort sitting cross-legged in the stacks of Sawyer, this was a distinction without a difference. The sculpture's erotic force was bound up with Proserpina's suffering, her vulnerability. She was to him no less desirable—indeed all the more so—for the fact that that desire was to her a violation—a kind of agony. This was unsettling news to Walter and, at the same time, liberating. Some notion of who he was was shown to be false and now he was free of it. Perhaps this was what Bernini or his patron—the Pope's dissolute nephew—had had in mind. Or perhaps it wasn't. But again, to Walter, this hardly mattered. Above his desk, he stuck a postcard of the rape. He called it, when his friends asked, the Truth about Walter. He met Florence just a few weeks later. Before he spoke to her, before he interrupted her work—she was busy sketching a line of trees—he had, quite deliberately, pictured to himself the god and his burden.

And yet, and *yet*, Pasolini can't give up on abstraction, Lopez told them.

When introduced to his fellow speakers the night before in the *salone*, Walter had felt they were, on the whole, an interesting group. Jurak from Penn had recounted stories from her childhood in Slovenia. Lopez, the burly modernist, had laughed and clutched his glasses and seemed vulnerable. Schnapp was, between drinks, brilliant on Fascist spectacle. Stark was young and sexy and happy with the power she exercised— glad, it seemed, to allow Lopez's—and Walter's—gaze to rest upon her.

So how to explain the current quandary? Lately, things at the conference had gone south. Jurak was evidently, even theatrically, bored. Lopez was stubborn, Schnapp smug, and Stark nasty. It was as if there were some potion in the coffee. He thought of Circe turning all of Odysseus' men into rams and chickens. Walter wondered what kind of claw or hoof he had sprouted. He actually glanced down at his feet.

The initial warning was a blood test. Walter's enzyme levels were, his doctor told him, anomalously high. Walter did not like to think about the inside of his body. Or, for that matter, anybody's body. He had had as a child a model of a transparent man whose organs could be removed and then reinserted through a detachable plate. The liver was surprisingly large and, even in its hard polystyrene form, disturbingly lumpish. He knew, roughly speaking, what the heart, the lungs, the kidneys, and the intestines did. But he kept forgetting why the liver was important, why you needed such an ungainly mass. His father had loved liver— specifically liver with grilled onions. When their half-savage Siamese was presented with a raw slab, the cat would attack it with joy.

Though his education was quite unwilling, Walter had come around. He now understood, now appreciated the liver. The body's biggest gland, it synthesized lipoproteins and coagulant factors, bile and cholesterol. It broke down insulin, ammonia, and bilirubin. Glucose, in the form of glycogen was stored in the liver, along with a two-year supply of vitamin A, a four-month supply of D, and three years' worth of B12. By some reckoning, the organ served in five hundred different metabolic functions. It was a master of many arts, a bit, Walter thought, like Bernini. He took out of his pocket a tube of pills, tapped into his palm a yellow and two blues, then downed them with a swig of water. He noticed Lopez, on the other side of the room, noticing.

Eventually, they went to Boston to meet a specialist, the wife—or maybe the cousin—of a former student. She laid out as kindly as she could the course of the disease, the stages and the options. I knew you would betray me, said Florence.

The sympathetic specialist had tried to explain that it was almost certainly a genetic abnormality, that it had nothing to do with lifestyle, that it was random, chance. Walter had merely taken Florence's hand and pressed it to his liver. I'm sorry, he said. I'm sorry.

Later, when they told Robert, he wept. Florence pressed him to her. Looking at mother and son in each other's arms, Walter felt already gone.

They let the news just trickle out and Walter could see that some of his friends were upset by this. One colleague, who went a long way back, took Walter aside.

You put people in a false position, he said. They act toward you as if things were just as they were and then they find out and they feel terrible and they feel angry. It matters whether someone is dying.

How does it matter?

If I were dying, you would take our conversation more seriously, you'd be more careful.

You *are* dying.

This is not a metaphysical point, Walter. This is not some abstraction. You are hurting people. And that's not OK just because you are dying.

But it was OK as far as Walter was concerned.

The discussion session broke up. Stark and Schnapp hung around the salone drinking coffee. Lopez and Jurak played a game of stripes and solids on the giant pool table. Walter retreated to his room. He hung his jacket on a chair by the window, lowered the blinds, and lay down on his bed, the sheets of which smelled of Italy. For his talk, Walter had chosen the title, "Fucking in Public: Art, Rape, Bernini." The organizers had politely demurred; and so it was listed in the conference proceedings as "Social Eros and the Methods of the Baroque." As usual, he had read the paper aloud to Florence, and she, as usual, had corrected his grammar, suggested cuts, pointed ways to tighten up his paragraphs. He could not resist asking her how she liked it, what she thought of the argument.

I'm not sure what you are after Walter; I'm never sure of what you are after. What's at stake in it for you? Why do you care?

It's what I do, he had said. I try to understand things, to make sense of them. You know this. What I want is to get inside another person's head—to enter their mind—Bernini's mind.

Bernini's dead, Walter.

In their early years together, each had worked independently from the other, as if that were the natural, the ordinary way for lovers, like travelers, to relate. Writing his first book—the book that took him every morning into the Raimondi chapel—he had taken Florence's disinterest for granted. One night, he had felt compelled to share an insight with her as they lay next to each other. Almost immediately she fell asleep. It became a joke with them, a ritual. On nights of insomnia, Florence would turn to Walter and say, tell me about Bernini. The one visit she made to the chapel had lasted three minutes.

Walter did not pretend to understand Florence's paintings. Florence herself did not understand them—or did not admit to doing so. When visiting artists would talk about the questions they were exploring in their work, when they would discuss their interventions, their reflections, their meditations, a hardness would appear around her eyes. Walter decided this was something that he admired in her, loved in her. But her rigor, her clarity, were not always easy for him, or for her. He was allowed to say that he liked particular canvases, but it was dangerous to go further. Paintings that he admired and that he thought Florence had finished would go back to the easel to be reworked until they ceased to resemble themselves. As the years went by, the number of paintings by Florence actually decreased.

Rome was like Florence, thought Walter as he lay in the darkened room. Every time you returned there, the city had been reworked and there was a bit less of it left. And yet still you kept coming back.

At least it's not from the cardinals, Schnapp grinned.

Walter had worried that things would only get worse, but he was wrong. After the break, Jurak delivered a paper on Guston's Roman interlude that was both original and, it seemed to Walter, right. There was a discussion—a real discussion—of the figurative turn in the painter's work. Then, during dinner, Schnapp told Pope jokes and Lopez again grabbed his glasses and laughed. Over *insalata di polipo e patate* and *Agnello alla Lucana* the group made peace, recovered its sense of humor, reclaimed the sense of privilege that comes with talking about art. Walter, of course, couldn't eat much or drink at all. But still he found it comforting, restoring. It occurred to him that this is why he had come—to sit at this meal, this last communion as it were.

During coffee, Stark had turned to him. I've been meaning to ask you, she said, about Emma Sulkowicz.

You mean the girl with the mattress.

I mean the artist with the mattress. Walter had followed the story because it was sensational, because it was moving. And because of the girl's gesture. The uncanny echo of it; the weird doubling.

What do you think? he had said to Florence after reading the piece that ran on the cover of *New York Magazine*. In protest against what she claimed was a rape, the girl, a college senior, was carrying around a mattress. One of the photos showed her hands digging into it. Is she thinking about Bernini?

Florence had been chopping onions. No, Walter, she had said, this is not an exercise in art history. She's not doing this for you. Or for Bernini.

But why couldn't she be thinking of Bernini? The god had picked up the girl—that gesture of his, that elevation, was, etymologically speaking, the essence of the violence. *Raptus*—from *rapere*—to be seized. Michelangelo, Carpi, Rubens, Rembrandt, they'd all done their Ganymedes, their Sabines, their Europas and Proserpinas. You couldn't get through Art 101 without being asked at some point to think about rape, to think about what the gesture signified.

Walter looked over at Stark. You want my reaction to the art or the politics of it?

Is there a difference?

In my view, and I know it's an old-fashioned view, there is a difference between rape and a picture of rape, between something real and something represented. You can't think clearly without drawing distinctions—did this happen or didn't it; is this a myth or a legal proceeding?

What if I told you I thought your interest in distinctions was an evasion, Stark answered, a way of avoiding something more basic, more essential? What if I said to deal with rape we've got to get past a preoccupation with thinking clearly that hasn't gotten us anywhere?

I'd say that you were wrong. That we had gotten somewhere. Here, in fact. Walter noticed the hard bright line of Stark's lipstick.

I'm sure, Walter, you know the figures on rape.

Walter almost pushed back, but then didn't. The aesthetics of rape, he said instead, are complicated. Because rape is, of course, a terrible thing—a terrifying thing. The question, again from an art historical perspective, is how we make sense of a particular painter's or sculptor's interest in it. That terror is easier, presumably, for a male artist to contemplate. And there is something ugly in that. There are certain acts that should, you could argue, not be made the subject of art except by those who are subject to them. But that's just another distinction and, historically speaking, not all that helpful. The works exist; we feel their power and their beauty.

Speak for yourself, said Stark. Then, unaccountably, she softened. The works you write about, Walter, you didn't paint them, you didn't sculpt them. As you say, they already exist. But when the lights go out and you flash up an image, and there is a woman in your audience who has been raped—and there is always a woman in your audience who has been—then you are showing it to her again. The power and the beauty of the image—how do they feel to her? How does your admiration of that power and beauty feel to her?

Lopez had been following the exchange and at this point decided to intervene. So no more paintings, no more Ledas and Danaes and Lucretias and Casandras?

Not by men.

And no more lectures? asked Walter.

Not by men. Stark smiled. After tonight. We are all looking forward—I'm looking forward—to hearing you. But you need to understand that what strikes you as harmless isn't necessarily going to seem so; it is not enough to say that you are well-intentioned. All the distinctions you invoke, between reality and art, art and scholarship, for the woman in the room who has been pushed on her back—or, yes, hoisted in the air—they all collapse. For her that luxury, that privilege of distance and clarity, is not an option.

But I'm not well-intentioned, said Walter. And neither was Bernini.

Much later, Walter woke to the sound of a nightingale. Perhaps because he was—or used to be—such an excellent sleeper, Walter knew the song only from what the poets had said of it. Listening hard in the darkness, he tried to make out in the trills and repeated phrases, the anguish and the longing, tried to hear the girl's tale of violation and dismemberment. He thought of Florence, who at this hour would be standing by the sink fixing herself a cup of tea, or sitting by the lamp in the living room ordering seeds, or lying in bed weeping.

Walter got up, dressed and, having been careful to take the key, made his way down to the garden. In the moonlight, he could distinguish the fruit trees, their blooms glowing, as well as the tall pines and their shadows. Even the massive villa had acquired a vagueness, an unreality. And all the while the bird kept singing, either moved by the beauty or, he thought, unmoved by it. Sweet, sweet, sweet, sweet, jug, jug, jug, jug, sweet, jug, jug, jug, jug.

If sculpture was a surface seen from the outside, then architecture, Walter liked to say, was a surface seen from the inside. You didn't walk around a building, you walked into it. It contained you, it held you. This was, of course, the theme of the vast colonnade that Bernini had conceived for St. Peters, the arms of the church reaching out and embracing—seizing—the bodies of the faithful. And this was how the two phases of Bernini's career connected. The young sculptor had begun with the god's view, which he claimed for himself and us. If while gazing on Proserpina's agony, you said that you were disturbed by it, that would be at best a half truth. You could not un-wish what was happening without denying the intensity, the immediacy of your pleasure. Whatever pity and anger the act elicited were subsumed in the delight, the wonder of the stonework. That was the godlike power of art, to be able to gaze on suffering—to grip it in your hands—without being touched by it.

In the corner of the garden where the Pope's battlement turned sharply stood a gate. Walter stepped through it, out of the Villa grounds and into Rome. He made his way down the hill past the great fountain, past the Fascist memorial to the dead, and up the steps of the church that contained the Raimondi chapel. The door that should have been locked gave way when Walter leaned on it. In the gloom, he found the illumination box and slid a euro into it.

Two weeks after Walter had been invited to Rome and a day before he had accepted, Florence had come to him with a magazine. She had laid it open on his desk. We could go here, she said.

It took Walter a moment to sort out what he was looking at.

The North Pole? he hazarded.

Greenland, said Florence. Ilulissat.

Walter looked again. There was nothing in the photograph to suggest a scale—no trees, no people, not even a rock. So a last vacation at the end of the world?

If you want to go somewhere, Florence said, I'll go with you, only not to stand in the same places, not to take in the same views.

In the photograph, the sky was reflected off the sea, the sea off the ice. It was sunset, or maybe dawn. Two icebergs were in shadow, a third, the largest, was in light. Its surface was lined with the channels formed by its own slow disintegration.

But this is just ice, Walter said.

The Raimondi were cardinals, wealthy and, in their conception of themselves, pious. Breaking radically with the practice of his time, Bernini depicted each man twice. Girolamo appeared on the left side of the chapel, engrossed in his breviary, unconscious of the corpse—his own corpse—lying beneath him in an open casket. Francesco, on the right, displayed the same indifference or obliviousness, but his gaze was turned outward, toward the church, toward Walter, as if he were surprised to find Walter there, as if the art historian were out of place. Walter stepped between the marble cousins and, knowing what he would see, looked up.

All of a sudden there was a dazzling light. It was as though the heavens were exploding and splashing forth all their glory in millions of waterfalls of colours and stars. And in the centre of that bright whirlpool was a core of blinding light that flashed down from the depths of the sky with terrifying speed until suddenly it stopped, motionless and sacred, above a pointed rock in front of Francis. It was a fiery figure with wings, nailed to a cross of fire.

*

Either Bernini or, more probably, one of the Raimondi had fixed on Francis' ecstasy as the chapel's theme. And the saint, like the cardinals, appeared twice within it. One version was sculpted in white marble, the other painted in polychrome—two views of the same transformative moment, the same visionary encounter, the same violent penetration.

As Francis uttered a mighty shout of joy and pain, the fiery image impressed itself into his body, as into a mirrored reflection of itself, with all its love, its beauty, and its grief. And it vanished within him. Another cry pierced the air. Then, with nails and wounds through his body, and with his soul and spirit aflame, Francis sank down, unconscious, in his blood.

The saint had prayed that he might know God's suffering and his love. Walter felt unsure of what he wanted. Did he want love at all or had he gone into art, had he married Florence to avoid it? It was very late to be asking such questions.

And since it was not clear there were answers, or if there were, that Walter wanted them, he returned his gaze to Francis, or to the two Francises in light and shadow and in color above his head.

Meadow

The butterfly is solar-powered;
it floats around the clearing, where the light is strong.

When it comes to the perimeter of shade, it turns,
and glides back into the clearing.

It doesn't use more energy than it requires,
and we have never seen a butterfly that kept on growing

bigger and bigger, from the size of an aspen leaf to a dinner plate.
No one ever noticed an insatiable butterfly

bulldozing down the acres of a field to build a new summer home,
or a butterfly superstore, where the butterfly

would sell imported pollen
to other butterflies at inflated prices.

I think you can see where I'm going with this.
I'm not going to drive the point like a nail into your head,

or take out an ad in the newspaper with your name on it
telling you to turn off the lights when you leave home,

or to donate all your money to the foundation for giraffes.
A poem should also be solar-powered,

and turn back at the edge of blame.
It should land on the tip of a yarrow-stalk

and then unfold its wings,
as light as a suggestion.

JAMES HOCH
The Singer

Some mornings, his father floats
at the foot of the stage
and asks him to sing. He knows
it is a ghost, a made

airy thing. He knows nothing,
no holler or raw shriek,
keeps his father out of ether.
Come, his shit-scared

rage song goes, *crawl into bed,
weight this body down.*
But the ghost just stands there,
taking it, nodding along,

letting the son's pain stay his,
white-knuckled at the mic.

DAVID HUTCHESON
Shank

A white cat, paranoid, inquisitive,
stalks night in circles around a white van with a shiv

of silver on its front. There's something secret
in the wheel-well. Her lovely feline shoulders roll as she paws it,

cocks her wild-eyed head at me, pretends to play with leaf rot
piled around the tire. The dumb alluring snub-nose box

economy of the van flaunts some convulsive engine
scent, outbids me for her attention.

There's something up there in the wheel-well
animal and dead and driving her to dance like hell

on the hood of the machine, batting at it, convulsing, a pallor
of sex strutting it out for no one in particular.

MARY KARR

Psalm for Riding a Plane

Tonight this silver plane is permitted
to bear me in its belly through a black wipe of sky.
And in the evil of my pride, I get
to forget I am You-formed—needlework of hair
stitched to my scalp growing outward,
stonework of bone, fret lines of tendon.
In this dark cabin, I fly strapped
in among other similarly shaved animals.
The round light above me is gray,
the stars outside like tack heads
holding up Your far off velvet. They foretell
fuck all. I place my palms together, fingers unlit
tapers invisibly burning for you.
Thirst is the truest knowledge of water.

CHRISTOPHER KENNEDY
Historical

Nothing moves me further away toward a mathematical horizon, completely abstract, like an oar-less boat on a perfectly still body of endless water, as when you speak to me in the fifty languages of nowhere. Though I have no answer, everything tastes like snow, a mineral sulk on the tongue, the essence of winter locked in every molecule. The wooly mammoth kissing his bride. A universe of ice embracing us. Everything beautiful and breathtaking. Almost wandering, we finally arrive. We build our nests that turn to stone. We make a wheel of fire. Then someone invents the word for bread; then horde; then empire. Look at us, we say. Then history begins.

PHILIP LEVINE
The Worst is Still to Come

If the express should slow and then
suddenly stop and sit utterly still
for minutes on end and all talk

stop and no one question the stillness,
no voice announce what, if anything,
is about to transpire (odd word, that,

for me, "transpire," out of Latin
"to go out into breath" or air or nothing),
and only I grow restive—the dozen

or so others drowsing or seemingly
at peace while the prophet on crutches
at last shuts his Bible and his mouth—

so that when I rise to stand the train
lurches forward to regain
its momentum and at last arrives

somewhere, a station on no map
I know, and I make my way upward
through the littered passageways

to where the street waits with no one
to welcome me, I'll know I'm home.

MAURICE MANNING
Thermopylae

It's unincorporated, but
there's a place in Kentucky called Burning Springs,
a few knobby hills and a stream
and the smell of rotten eggs in the air.
An unlikely place for paradox,
but there it is, mysteriously,
the ground is oozing paradox.
If it was ever the scene of valor
it's unrecorded, which I prefer.
What's so impressive about a bunch
of people dying needlessly?
And we've sort of bent the rules when it comes
to valor; as with many things,
we've tended to exaggerate.
Isn't courage a private matter,
that doesn't crave recognition?
And I've been getting tired of all
the Classical allusions—they're too,
uh, Classical, a little too
highfalutin for my taste.
It's funny, all the Spartans are gone,
and the Greek warriors devoted
to Demeter or one of the other gods—
outnumbered and overrun by the Persians, who,
ironically, are also gone,
along with Persia itself. Persia
is gone from the maps. It's hard to believe.
And the ancient city-state of Sparta.
I remember being very confused
in school on all the city-states
and who was aligned with whom and why,
they never seemed too civilized
to me. But I was a bad student,

looking out the windows at trees
and doing a lot of daydreaming.
I've always liked the civilization
of trees and the gray-green, hoary
assembly of hills, the wordless meaning,
the silent assent of trees and hills.

KATHRYN MARIS
The A Man

His superpower was achieving the world's first happy marriage
by wedding his daughter, whom he loved at first sight
i.e., when she was adopted at the age of 6 by the woman
he was wooing & whose inevitability in the girl's life
led him to stick around until the girl was a preteen, a reedy
netball-star-in-the-making whose long legs under her
polyester shorts gave him a semipermanent hard-on
that he translated into practiced looks of empathy & affection
which all girls need to properly grow & so she grew
to adore this man like a New Testament God & it came to pass
that once of legal age, she entered his sagging bed & stayed there.

DAVID TOMAS MARTINEZ
Falling

Nobody judges
clumsiness, and nothing about
      wounded animals

makes me weep,
      but something about
a woman with eyelashes

like broken wings, about a woman
      wearing leopard print
who wears the smell of death,
languidly   awaiting   a predator

that makes the slow descent
      of stairs, into flame, from alley,
     into club, more than just a room
of throbbing light, more than
entering a cave, decorating bone.

DONNA MASINI
Waiting Room

Your sister's inside in a green gown
and you, here, twisting your dread into origami
tissues, riot mind ticking *wrong wrong*,
you've crashed your mooring,
fear every wart, organ, every minor—
what's this pain in my groin?
Is this what's been waiting
all along? All of us carried off on a train,
pressed to a window, charting the crazy migration
of cells, disaster oaring
steadily after us like magi
to the babe. And time, grim monitor,
screening each of us in our green toga.
One day you're drinking your first martini,
a minute later you're roaming
some hospital wing—(Why call it a wing?
Why say origami when it's a useless rag?)—
Now none of it matters. Not your iron
will, your impeccable timing.
You think of a far-off war-torn town
hiding your sister in her twin gown.

JAMAAL MAY

Things That Break

Skin of a plum. Rotting tooth.
Switches cut down by a child

to lash a child's legs.
A siege does something like this

against sturdy walls. The wrong rules.
A dozen angel figurines flying

from a balcony. Flailing fist. Splint.
Forefinger and index,

dislocated, not broken. One points
to the left of a man

and the rubbery thing inside quivers
familiar. Raise your hand

if you know how to do this.
If enough hair fails to escape

the pull of a drain and the drain
sputters and fails to swallow water

we will say it is broken. Waves.
Traffic lights. The craven infantry

of roaches at the flick of a switch.
Will. A child in a shrinking living room
sitting more still than the father.

NATHAN MCCLAIN
To Have Light

Somewhere on I-5, in the flash of hazard lights,
I was broken-down. But it seemed enough to have light.

The piano playing itself in the hall needs
tuning, its notes ghostly and bent in the half-light.

Tennis shoes and tin cans tied to the car the couple
rushed out toward, struck by rice and the sun's grave light.

Before sorrow was the garden, the man and woman,
the tree—forbidden. Before sorrow, God gave light.

Orpheus repeats his great sin of looking back...
Is it memory—*regret*—calling from the cave's poor light?

She walked with the brilliance of a sequined dress. How
could I ignore such shimmer, such provocative light?

Then, the birds attended her: seagulls circled and wailed.
And on the telephone line, the mourning doves alight.

"*When the one they were expecting came into the room...*" Then,
there—Nathan, a flame in their eyes: they were slaves to his light.

TAYLOR KOEKKOEK
Emergency Maneuvers

We three brothers spent the afternoon outside in the haze and half rain. We trekked the empty field out behind the decommissioned paper mill where our father used to work and we were fallen upon by ashes from Mount St. Helens, which had erupted three days ago, and once more two days after. Though the wind took most of the ashes east, as far they said as Oklahoma, there was still the gray silt here, and the car's tread through it on the roadways like a snow dusting. It looked like the beginning of the end of the world. This was March of 1980 in Oregon. Spring drizzling turned the ash to a fine black mud, which stole the petrichor from the air, and the earth smelled as if the grass and the trees and overgrowth would stop growing for good. I imagined that we would live out our lives in these gray ruins, and we would describe someday to children of our own how the world had looked when there was still green in the hills and red poppy blossoms on the shoulder of the highway, and blackberry bramble winding down to the runoff pond near the overpass where we had once seen nutria loitering in the mud and the cattails.

Carson, who was fifteen and the oldest of us, found a wooden boomerang beneath an ashy clump of grass, which he tore free and tucked into the back of his jeans as though it were a pistol. He hiked on, up over the low rocks and beneath us: the earth rolling down to a gray wasted farmland, and a gray distance farther on.

"Throw it, then," Denny said, who was ten—the youngest of us. He always wore shorts and spent a good deal of our outings tending thorn pricks on his shins.

"No," Carson said.

"Why not?"

"If it doesn't come back, I may not find it again." He waved his arm out at the impenetrable thickets of blackberry vines.

And I said, "If it doesn't come back, then it's broken anyway."

"It isn't broken," Carson said, and untucked his shirt from behind the boomerang so that we could only see the outline of it beneath the fabric. Carson had a bruise on his cheek, which he'd returned with one afternoon after school and said nothing about.

Our house was small, though our property was enough to house two cars that our father had long planned to get running again, and an old 125cc dirt bike, which was rusted out, and then behind the shed, beneath a black tarpaulin, our father's Ford Ranger, which was in danger of repossession. Our mother's new absence robbed the home of its warmth. Perhaps some of that, too, was the bit of ash hung in the air, and in windrows below the door.

Our mother had been, for the last week, an hour south in Coburg with our grandmother and our uncle and with our grandfather who was dying. Our grandfather never liked our father. We knew this even then because our father never hid it. "I'll be civil if he is," our father would say, which meant that no one would be civil. What frightened me most was not the idea of our grandfather dying—my brothers and I never knew him all that well—but the sense that his death might change our mother so that she would become less like our mother.

She said grandfather saw skyscrapers where there were not skyscrapers. When he was driven through the one-story neighborhoods of Coburg, our grandfather had rested his head against the windows and said, "I know they're not really there."

"Maybe he's just seeing the future," our father said later. "Maybe you're fussing over nothing."

"There is no future," she said, "however distant, where Coburg, Oregon, is a thriving metropolis."

"Who knows?"

"Coburg will get smaller every day and one day it'll dry up and blow away in the wind. He's dying. I don't expect you to care."

"All right."

"I wish you'd care for my sake at least."

"Sure," our father said. "I wish that too." He finished his beer and our mother went to bed and we three brothers listened through our door, cracked only enough to let in the muffled ghosts of their voices and a slip of light, which bent along the wall and caught Denny's pupil so that it lit up like a cat's.

We were here behind the paper mill, which was in the process of being torn down, and the jagged metal innards of it, exposed, reminded me of a very large ship with the hull broken off. Our father had worked on the floor on machine number two. When they shut the plant down, first they'd shipped off what machinery they could sell. Great rows of trucks carted it all away, and our father said to us—as he traced the procession's path down the highway—"I've turned every screw on that machine twice." I think he was more familiar with the press and the rollers than he was with our mother. It was only once that I crept into the kitchen in the morning and saw my father behind my mother, with his arms around her waist and his chin on her shoulder. It was only that one time, and so I have kept this memory close. Father used to come home with grease-black hands and go immediately to the sofa, where he'd sit, for a moment, with his boots still on.

Now, with the mill gone, father and the other mill workers were like some generation of orphan children. He haunted his own home, and did not know what to say to us who lived there. He woke early in the blue-black mornings, and in the afternoons, we watched him pass in and out of the room and then in again, as though there'd been something he'd meant to do, except he could not remember what it was.

We stood there in the ash fall and listened to the distant sound of the last few tinkerers in the mill, stripping the copper piping and wires and throwing it all in dumpsters. These were its last days and the sun was already setting, and we were there on the other side of the fence.

That morning, I'd sat outside alone to watch the sun come up through the tree, as I often did, and I saw, across the yard, between two unkempt blueberry bushes, a deer, standing like the statue of a deer, which ran off after a moment that felt much longer than it was. There was ash in its fur. The image occurred to me periodically throughout the day, and sometimes even still, and yet there seemed to be very little to say about it, so I never mentioned it to my brothers—the deer and the ash and how it seemed to come to life.

Denny was the first to catch the sound of a motor approaching. Our father's pickup climbed the hill and tossed up a small rooster tail of ash.

"He's coming," Carson said.

"What do you figure for?" Denny said.

Carson shrugged. "Us, I guess."

I said maybe the repo man was snooping around again. Our father had, for a time, parked the pickup on the edge of Shelby's lot, beneath a gathering of plum trees, which Shelby had neglected, so that the fruit grew and fell and was lost in the weeds, where hornets burrowed into it and came out too sticky to fly. Eventually, Shelby noticed our father coming and going on his land and told him he could rent the spot. Since then, he'd begun parking again on our lot, behind the shed. We'd been instructed to keep watch for tow trucks cruising the area.

With his elbow out the window, our father called to us, "Hey, boys. Come on. We're going out for a while."

Denny and I climbed around the passenger seat into the foldout seats in back, and Carson sat up front, since his legs were too long to fit in back. He untucked the boomerang from his belt. The windshield wipers on low squealed and dragged black smears across the glass, and the upholstery smelled warmly of stale cigarette smoke.

"Where we going?" Denny said.

"Where do you want to go?" our father said.

Denny shrugged and looked out the window.

"We'll just go out for a bit." He put the truck in gear. "We'll go for a drive. My father used to take the family out for a drive every Sunday." He looked at us all in the rearview mirror and said, "All right," and then we drove off. As we passed the mill our father only said, "Sad thing, isn't it?"

We brothers were just learning how to spend time around our father. After this many years of life, we'd become familiar only with the sound of his footsteps down the hall in the night, and in the mornings a cup of cold coffee on the end table and the newspaper draped over a sofa arm, as though moved there by a bleary-eyed poltergeist. Today we found ourselves riding in the cab of his truck as though in the company of a stranger, although one who held some insight into our creation and our future.

There had never been such a thing as a forty-hour workweek at the mill. After every shift, father and the other men blew off an hour or two at the Golden Nugget Tavern to prepare themselves for home life, whether the shift had ended at seven in the evening or seven in the morning. Sometimes our mother had trouble sleeping and she'd load us up in the car for a night drive. We wore winter coats over our pajamas and rolled slowly by the mill lot until one of us could spot out father's pickup, which she made into a game for us, and once it was played and won, we would return home. Only one time were we unable to spot the pickup, and she did not sleep that night.

Our father traded glances between us in the mirror and the road.

"Listen, boys," he said. "Your mother called today. She said your grandfather died this morning. I don't know much more than that."

We were quiet. Our father turned off toward the little city center.

"Does that mean mom will be coming home?" I asked.

"Soon, Levi," our father said. "She's not ready just yet. But she'll be back."

"She say when?" Denny said.

"No, but she won't be long."

Our father noticed the old boomerang on Carson's lap.

"What do you got there, Carson?"

"A boomerang. Found it behind the mill."

Father looked at it for a few moments and nodded. "Think you're a little old for that?"

Carson shrugged.

"Why don't you give that to your brothers."

Carson tightened his grip on the toy and looked at our father.

"Go on," our father said. He studied Carson's bruise for a moment.

Carson lowered his eyes and handed the boomerang to Denny, who took it and looked at me as though for direction. He sat with it in his lap, with his hands not even touching it. We went on in silence.

"How about milkshakes, huh?"

He turned on to the main street, which extended for no more than seven or eight blocks, with the Snowcap near the center. Our father rarely offered these sorts of luxuries, and even more rarely in the recent months of his unemployment, so we betrayed no reaction for fear that he had misspoken, or that we had misunderstood. Still he parked alongside the curb and twisted the keys from the ignition and said, "Well, come on already." The ash-covered street and street side were empty except for a few lonely men with their hands in their pockets, walking as if they had somewhere to be.

We tracked in gray footprints, and a small gray gust, and a bell above the door sounded. I had been here before, once, but not for what felt like a very long time. The booths were empty and the jukebox was playing and the walls were surfaced with wood paneling. There was a Coca Cola glass-door refrigerator behind the counter full with sodas, and in the bottom, in a cardboard box, a pile of tomatoes.

"Ah," said a mustachioed man at the counter. "A few souls brave enough for this doomsday weather." There was a girl behind him with an apron and a shy look about her, playing, it seemed, with some trinket in her pocket. She looked as though she might have been Carson's age.

"It'll take more than some ash to keep us home," our father said.

"So it seems," the man said. "What'll you have?"

"Chocolate milkshakes. All around," he said. "Except not for me."

We sat at a booth by the window and followed the ash through the orange light of the streetlamps. We watched the second-floor windows of Main Street for the shapes of people passing behind the glass. Carson flicked away a flake of ash that had caught in Denny's lashes.

The restaurant girl brought us three milkshakes on a yellow tray and said, "Here you are." Carson said thank you and watched her pass back behind the counter and disappear behind the kitchen machinery. Carson stared for a while and then mixed his milkshake with the straw.

"Talk to her, then," our father told him.

Carson said, "Huh?"

"We see you watching her. Go talk to her."

"Why?" he said. "No." And then he took to drinking his milkshake as though it required his total focus.

"Carson—" Our father crammed his knuckles into his pocket and pulled out some money. "Actually, I would like a milkshake. Go order for me, would you? Just a small one. And don't you let her bring it over here. You wait there for it."

Carson looked at the money and then took it and made a fist of it. Our father caught his sleeve. "I want you to tell her your name. All right? It doesn't matter if she doesn't tell you hers. You tell her yours." Carson paused and then he nodded and went off.

Father and I watched him at the counter rubbing the back of his neck, and though we could hear his voice, we couldn't quite hear the words. She was a quiet, pretty thing. Redheaded and freckled and miniature in her proportions. I knew only that girls were pretty, but I hadn't any idea what to do with them. And then I noticed, and father after me, that Denny had picked a scab on his shin and he had a bit of blood on his fingers, which he was using to draw a stickman into the plastic, yellow back pad to the booth.

"Hey, Denny," our father said sternly.

Denny snapped to and looked at father with big eyes, as though waking from a trance. He looked at the blood on his fingertips. Denny held them up for us to see, pushing his thumb and index finger together and pulling them apart, which made a small, tacky noise.

"Christ, Denny," our father said. "People eat here." He sighed and massaged the bridge of his nose with his fingers. "All right. Go wash up. Get on." Denny hopped from the booth and dashed off to the bathroom.

"Christ," father said as he scooted out of the booth and to the other side where Denny had sat. "Dirty creature." He pulled a napkin from the dispenser and spat on it and scrubbed away Denny's little blood man. Then he looked at me and smiled wearily. We sat like this for a while and I drank my milkshake.

"Where'd Carson get the shiner?" he asked.

I shrugged.

"He didn't say anything about it?"

"No."

"You ask him?"

"No."

He turned his attention to the window, where he watched the ash through his reflection.

"You might be the quietest kid in the world, Levi," he said.

I thought about this. "Maybe."

"Well you shouldn't be, not if you can help it any. A man needs to be able to demand things of the world. Otherwise—I don't know. Otherwise it'll roll over you."

I felt very small then, and yet I was thrilled even so by the wholeness of my father's attention. I said nothing because it seemed too much to begin speaking now.

"Ah," our father said. "Maybe you shouldn't bother listening to me. I could've probably kept a few things to myself and been better for it. Maybe it's better to wish you'd said something than to regret saying something you shouldn't have. Maybe it'll all weigh on you just the same. Who knows? Never mind. Don't listen to me."

There are these moments when something about your own life—the course and nature of it—is revealed before you're ready for it, which leaves you braced as though against a force incoming from an unknown direction, like this: like me in a booth in the Snowcap with the jukebox playing a song I didn't know.

Carson returned, put a milkshake in front of our father, and said, "I told her my name."

"Did you?"

"And she told me hers."

"And what was it?"

"It started with a J," he said, and smiled. He went to his milkshake.

"J?"

"She was quiet. It was a good name, but it was hard to hear exactly what she said."

Our father laughed and said, "That's something, I guess." And then he drank his milkshake too and looked at it and seemed to think about it.

When Denny returned, father made him show us his hands and his legs, and when father was satisfied with his cleanliness, he let him sit down. Denny was the first to ask about mother again, and our father said, "I told you, she didn't say when she'd be back. For all I know, it may be tonight. She may be on her way already. I can imagine that."

Knowing that it was possible, despite the way it felt in our guts, was some sort of relief. We brothers smiled. I imagined my mother's hands.

As we drove away, father told us about an old man who had refused to leave his house on Mount St. Helens and who had died there by a lake, which was vaporized along with him. He was one of the two people killed by the eruption. As they considered the man's motives I sat there wondering about what my father had tried to tell me in the Snowcap—about the weight of words spoken and unspoken, which was not a weight I understood. And did that weight accumulate? I imagined then the weight my father seemed to collapse with into a sofa, and the heaviness of his footfalls through the hall, and the hunch of his shoulders up a set of stairs. No, it did not make sense to me, so I sat there playing absently with my hands.

We didn't go straight home then. Maybe this was because there was a repo man still snooping around the property, or because we imagined the longer we stayed away, the more likely it was that mother would be there when we arrived. And yet we had nowhere else to go. As if by instinct, father drove us to the paper mill. He parked in the empty lot, situated with our backs to the road, and facing the broken shape of the mill hulking in the dark. He said. "I want to teach you boys something.

Pay attention back there." He wrenched an elbow over the seat. "Here's the thing: you may be the best driver in the world, but your car can still fuck you. Or foul you up. Don't tell your mother I'm swearing. You need to know how to handle yourselves in an emergency." He put the pickup in neutral and stepped out and said into the cab, "Trade me, Carson."

Carson could drive manual. He used to move the car around to help father with chores. They stepped out into the semilit lot and exchanged a few words in the headlights. Father put a hand on Carson's shoulder and said something and looked directly into Carson's eyes, and then they parted and Carson climbed into the driver's seat.

"All right. What happens if you've got a stuck accelerator?"

Carson looked at our father and then checked the pedals and said he didn't know.

"Imagine the truck is speeding up and up."

"All right."

"What's the first thing you do?"

Carson seemed unsure of the question itself, as though he were trying to discern our father rather than an answer, and as he sat there looking at him, Denny called out, "Hit the brakes."

"Right," our father shouted. "And then what? Say you speed up even more." He waited and got tired and answered, "If you speed up when you hit the brake, it means you've been hitting the gas instead by accident. So take your feet off the pedals. And check—make sure the floor mat hasn't wedged the pedal down."

"OK," Carson said.

"You boys get that back there?" our father said over his shoulder. "Now let's say there's a real malfunction with the throttle and you weren't just being dumbasses. So you keep going faster, even with feet off the pedals. Put her in gear, Carson."

Carson put the shifter into first and waited.

"I shouldn't have said that—about being dumbasses," Father said. "We all do dumbass things occasionally and that's all right." He surveyed the lot and then he said, "Denny, I'm going to let you out. You see the push cart there?"

"Yeah."

"Move that out of the way."

"Where to?"

He thought about this as he got out so that Denny could exit from behind the seat, and he said. "I want you to push the cart as hard as you can that way." He pointed. Denny looked at him and smiled, and our father said, "That's right. Hard as you can."

We laughed wildly when Denny set up behind the cart, which was loaded with a stack of copper piping, and threw all his strength into it. The cart went rattling and caromed off a curb and let a few pipes loose and clattering into the other aisle of the lot. Denny was quiet, and then he held his arms up triumphantly and our father hooted.

"All right already," our father shouted. "Get back in here." Denny ran back and clambered in, and our father said, "OK, buckle up then. OK. Good, you're in first. In a moment here I want you to gun it. Get to the top end of second, you got that."

"Gun it?"

"Like a lead foot, Carson. And when I say so, throw her in neutral and start braking. You can do that?"

Carson paused and smiled and said that he thought so.

"And listen, when you brake, don't slam on it. You hit the brake all the way and we'll lock up. Once you've locked her up, we go skidding and there's no steering anymore. Keep your heel right there on the floor—good—and ease on just until the tires squeal. No howl though. Just a squeal. You ready? Don't think too much."

Carson, with his hands trembling on the wheel, nodded. I wanted to hug Denny in excitement. Our father clicked his seatbelt in place.

Father shouted, "First," and Carson let out the clutch and hit the throttle. Father shouted, "Second," and Carson lurched into second. The lot, which had seemed so much larger in the disuse of the night, collapsed on us, whirring us by lamppost and lamppost, and through a series of shadows. "Neutral," father shouted. "Brake. Yes!" He pounded joyously on the dash and shouted, "Yes!" Denny was clapping and hip hollering in the dark of the cab as we came to rest in a gray-black cloud, which lit up nearly white in the headlights, hung there for a moment, and dissipated.

Father breathed deeply and regained himself and then, smiling over his shoulder at us, he asked, "And what if you can't get to neutral? What then?"

"Do we get to do it again?" Denny asked.

Carson was patting his fingers lightly on the wheel. "Then you have to kill the engine," he said.

Kill! What a word. We considered it for a moment—how it rattled in the heart.

"That's right," our father said. "We'll do it again. But now the clutch is out. The shifter is shit. Kill the engine. Get up to the top of second again. Denny, are you still buckled? Levi, make sure he's buckled."

I said he was.

"Carson, you know what it means when I say power brakes?"

Carson looked at the brake pedal and shook his head.

"Means that, once the engine's off, the brakes lose most of their juice. That's what the emergency brake is for." He patted beneath the dash at the emergency pedal and he slapped Carson's knee. "You see that?" Carson saw it. "When I tell you to kill it, hit the clutch, go to neutral, turn the ignition, and push the emergency brake. You won't be able to steer much with the engine off. This is a last resort. You got that?" Carson went over the steps once more aloud, then he pulled the truck around into the aisle as if it were a runway. We stared ahead into streetlamp haze and felt our pulses clicking in our necks. Even then our mother was washing her father's deathbed sheets, and the truck already belonged to the bank, and ash was raining from the sky. "Go," our father shouted. "Go, go go!"

And we went.

MICHAEL MCFEE
Yardsticks

Skinny printed boards
half ad, half measurement,
they came home with dad
from businesses he visited,
their names and numbers
and *Lowest Prices!* slogans
branded into cheap wood
like on giveaway pencils.
Lightweight, I'd wield one
as a bat, a sword, a club:
if it splintered, no problem,
there were plenty of trees
and we could find more,
it was like taking toothpicks
when leaving a restaurant.
Three times the foot-length
of any grade-school ruler,
they helped mom measure
her two kids' progress up
the kitchen door's jamb,
our time-lapse marathon
to an overhead finish line,
each height noted in pencil
at semiannual intervals:
at first I was a fraction taller
than the 36 wooden inches
from a furniture store,
and beanpole older sister
towered over little brother,
but years later I passed her
during a teen growth spurt.
Then the markings stopped.
I'm the last one vertical:

they lie side by side by side
two dark yardsticks down
in the hilltop graveyard.

JAMES MCMICHAEL
Exchange

          I answer the phone.
After the usual delay,
no telemarketing hum but a male-voiced

"Gotcha,

gotcha a little bit."
His tone is practiced.
It boasts he's finalized
everything that needed saying.
Here in me to be jeered at is the thing we've

all got coming that may not end well.
I hang up
gotten a little,
go back to being gettable,

on call.
(Two months ago I deferred jury duty.

A machine will tell me soon I'm wanted in court.)

It's projected that in not many years,
there will be fewer of us
dead than alive. All of us,
so far,

are either
dead or on call.
He didn't know me from Adam.
He learned from my "Hello" that I wanted him to be
heard from. He obliged.

The Red Umbrella

Of the stiff-backed prime minister the people said
That he had swallowed his umbrella. They trusted him
Not with their lives, their daughters, or their pension plans,
But with something intangible: his bloodshot eyes
Glimpsed in their collective souls a yearning to undo
The code by which they lived—the code he would rewrite
In a war launched on an imaginary foe.

———————

The doctor rubbed her stethoscope to warm it up
Before she listened to the girl's clogged lungs. *Forgive me,*
She said. *Take a deep breath.* The child began to cough.
And then they saw an older woman through the window
Opening an umbrella. Rain was not expected
Until nightfall, and so this splash of red against
Grey sky reduced the doctor and the child to giggles.

———————

The red umbrella in the hall of statues carved
From marble quarried in the Cyclades and sold
To merchants from Smyrna—this was how we knew
The war was almost over. There were figs in the market,
The roads were passable again, and the bells ringing
Hourly in the churches stopped. *In the beginning,*
The condemned man said in his cell. *Lucky me.*

JOSEPH MILLAR
The Poetry-Body

for Kwame Dawes

The youngest won't fall asleep
though he keeps resting his head on the table
next to his empty plate.
These are the jewels of his
half-open eyes bewitched by the pale
blossoming spines of the centerpiece flowers
no one remembers the names of—
these are the sparks flying up
from the fire and the dark
pressing in on the windows.

I know by now the harsh stillness
of a winter night by the beach,
the moon half hidden
low and dim
and sometimes I think
poetry has failed me,
the nights gone by and chances missed
all breathing deeply beside me—
"a fluttering of feathers"
you called it
this soft body that consumes everything
especially our failures
carrying something under its tongue
it is not going to show
to anyone.

CAROL MOLDAW
Confessional

Red tinsel wrapped around a roadside cross
glints in the sun like a cop's strobe bar,
then recedes into the drive's unbroken trance.

Power lines X-Acto-knife the sky.
Pasted and scraped, a billboard's pastel
palimpsest, photographed in raking light.

Our eyes locked on the road, stories unpeel
in the rental car's souped-up and streamlined
confession box. Stripped of penance and shame,

some of what we say exhaust drowns out,
some's keenly heard. Above sandstone cliffs,
low-level clouds mop up the sun's spillover—

or is that the sun dabbing at the clouds'
sniffed-back tears? Tell me a bizzaro factoid
that implicates yourself. See if I swerve.

HONOR MOORE
Night Café

Who rhymes
Knives with sight?
Watches horror late at night?

Across the way
He phones and orders wine.
As diners dine

The knife cuts back
To a skirt.
A hand there never hurt.

The bark hello:
Is it me who first goes blank?
Cannot greet or thank

Him at my ear?
Silent goes the phone.
A knife hits bone.

TOMÁS Q. MORÍN
For My Daughter

Even after I add up all your birthdays
I've celebrated but that haven't come
to pass since that day long ago when we agreed
it would be better if you never drew that
first breath of air, you're still only zero,
as all the unborn are, though you never look
like a zero, which resembles the eye of a needle
or even less than that, the head of a needle
maybe, though that also seems too large,
which doesn't matter because I always see you small
and running (at what age does that happen?)
across a porch toward my arms
that for once aren't filled with books or groceries
or even the arms of a lover and as you
draw closer I see your brow is sweaty
because you've been pretending you're a cowboy again
as you like to do, and that I'm a buffalo
stabbed and shot so many times it doesn't know
it's already dead and so it keeps on
limping around while you chase away
the buzzards it thinks are pretty
and so round and round our little game goes
until you get tired of playing the hero, throw
away your star, and face my shaggy frown
just before you smile and jump
back home in between my horns.

We Have Reasons for Wanting to Mend the Known World:

plank by plank a footbridge begins in thought
where over gaps ideas will walk their way toward order.

Light blue paint between the wings of gray moths
weighted down by dew on a morning wall

and grounded by a lust for a night light:
it looks pretty, all this intractable trouble.

We want the facts and need a fact checker
who can call us on our kettle of velvet:

when she utters kinetic words like
freight and *teal* and *flight*

just to warm up her mind,
she's using a lonely word in her best voice.

It's a practice she's been preaching
like faraway old friends more beautiful when out of reach.

The fog burning off into day reveals a larger world
of visibility granted and none of it our doing—

and so we need a sun for our bidding and our burning.
Poets talk in testimony from complicity

and the moth-light touch of intentions,
provided we care for people more than art.

JOHN MURILLO
Uptown Saturday Night

After Ernie Barnes, Sugar Shack, circa 1971

Here, says a card shark spreading a map, are the rest
of your days laid out. Of course, the lines are faded.
The valleys, now, overgrown with havoc and industry,
the seven unnamable roads rubbed to faint music
in the back of an old man's mind. Was there a town
there? A woman he once loved? The lights go dim
and the band strikes up. But loneliness, you think,
is its own small city. A gravedigger sidles up, offers
to pay for your dinner. I'm drinking it, you say,
then bank a *bang me* look off the dusty mirror floating
over the barhop's shoulder, to the one-armed drummer
grinning from the bandstand. He's in the pocket.
He's getting down. His hand is a blur of bad intentions
when he blows you six kisses. You uncross
and cross your legs. I run a sanctuary for out of work
morticians, the gravedigger says. Of course, you ignore
the gravedigger. Just like you ignore the four drunk
church ladies glaring from the cheap seats, and hike
your skirt just a little bit more. An oil lamp sputters
on every table in the joint. Reflected near every flame,
a crooked gold tooth. You check the bandstand again,
try to catch the drummer's eye. But he's eyeing thighs
on the other side of the room. Shorter skirt, skinnier
waist on a younger, faster, you.   If loneliness, Lady,
is an old world city, tonight you plan to be mayor.
All the walls sweat when the lights come up. Last call,
and the gravedigger's disappeared with your pocketbook.

SHARON OLDS
Ode to the Glans

I know—why did I wait until now,
the last moment, almost the moment
after the last moment, to sing
to you, outermost, tender, heart.
Respect held me back, and shyness.
Before I first saw you, I had not
seen even a picture of you, and you were
fearsome—when it would come down to it,
between you and my maidenhead,
I knew I could trust you to push until I was
torn from my virginity—
and you were adorable, you and the penis
like the dearest most basic doll, you were like
a brain without a skull, you were like
a soul. When I was eye to eye,
for the first time, with you, and I saw you
weep, the gleaming tear emerge
from the top of your mind, from your fontanelle,
I saw how it was going to be—it was
going to be what the movie in the dark of the
blossoming flower had promised, the rich
spongy corolla, the firm male
softness, it was going to be
mercy, and ecstasy—and, in there,
there were real babies, tiny, fresh,
with tinier babies inside them, enough
to last a lifetime, and beyond a lifetime, and a lifetime.

KATIE PETERSON
Note to Self

Why are you so hard
on the suicide
like self-love is his only
problem not getting the position
of his body right
in front of the train?
Full sun. The mirror in the hotel
actually a television set, no one
here to make a commentary
to, last night, you sat
next to the brother
in law of the famous
woman television
commentator on the plane.
He tells you about his college days.
As they do, men
of a certain age,
daughterliness still
quickening instead
of a child on your face.
A girl he never picked up
in college didn't
understand the plain
sense of how the horizon
never doesn't make
a circle. Seems
he could have said
the same for the soul, the builders
of the cathedrals
did, their mandates in floor
plans realized in stone.
When he asked your name,
he said his first.

Isn't this the way. When Stephen
Gregory stepped onto the track
in front of what
came next some dumb
thought made him do that.
Let's kill the thought.
Next time let's.

EMILIA PHILLIPS
Static, Frequency

A lash across the bandwidth bedstead—
my radio superego led by *heel, toe, dosey
doe*. Memories aren't
mercy, even if they rescue
you into innocence. I wish it wasn't easy
for the body to think I've suffered
because I sweat in front of a gym TV
on which St. Louis police
draw on another young man. Because I wince,
because I'm grateful
there's no sound, because empathy
is always a bad overdub, don't
trust me. I'm running
from no one. On the closed
captioning: [*man shouting*] OH
MY GODD! This is America,
where few witness
and most watch. I keep
running toward it
without ever getting there.
[*static*] Nights
I listened to that station in my twin
bed, country had nothing
to do with land but with
boundaries. Silence was
an inheritance I didn't know
I'd received. Did I sing
for my father & his cop
buddies *bullets* & *My-babies*?
Officers, I'm getting
nowhere. Officers, I have to
know: would you have fired?
Would my father? I sang

at the dinner table: *get down, turn
around.* I knew the words then
but didn't (didn't I?)
know the song.

SORAYA PALMER
Walk Like a Man

First, some disclaimers:

I know what you're thinking. Where does Sasha Porter, otherwise known as the Family Pariah, get off thinking she can pull it together long enough to tell you a story? That it should be my sister, Zora the Great, telling this story. Zora, the writer; Zora, Daddy's favorite. Yes, that Zora. But, this is my story too. I'll be telling you this story the way I remember it, which is to say it'll be all over the place. I'm really not the storyteller that Zora is, so you'll just have to bear with me. There'll be no drawn-out metaphors here. None of that sentimental shit. I'm gonna tell it like it is.

9/18/1999: Four Weeks Before the Baby Comes and Changes Everything

So this is about two weeks after Mom spins this elaborate bedtime story—the one where Dad's in Europe on "business" for like the umpteenth time. Dad still calls every week or so saying, yeah, he'll be back to see Zora star as Anacaona in the school play, yeah he'll be back to talk to my teachers and find out where all this "back sliding" behavior's been coming from. Yeah, I heard Mom yelling at him on the phone about missing parent-teacher conferences. He didn't want to talk to me. Don't worry, it's not like I care to be sitting behind those rose-colored lenses. Don't want that kind of attention right now. Have plans to formulate and all that. With the new baby coming at any moment, there isn't much space in the house. Even with my own room, I still have Zora bugging me like every five minutes for everything: *What does it feel like to be kissed? What does it feel like to be a woman? What does it feel like to drink beer in the park with high-school girls and not get caught?* Zora doesn't get that I'm really not into all that. We used to be like two peas. But in the last few weeks, even she hasn't seen that I'm changing—that I need my space.

9/21/1999: Dad's Wardrobe

My favorite room in the house is Dad's office. Mom put all his clothes and stuff in there so that she doesn't have to sleep with it every night.

That'd be my guess. She had me help her move his entire dresser and medicine cabinet into his office. No one goes in there except for me. I go in there two, three times a week in between doing homework or running errands for Mom when she's lying on the sofa in the baby's room watching *Matlock* and Zora's off in space obsessing over some boy who barely acknowledges her existence or some other dumb shit.

See, my father's office is like this gold mine. It even has its own bathroom with cabinets and mirrors and stuff. I have this whole ritual I go through every time I'm there. First, I sift through his work sweaters: Calvin Klein crew necks modeled after the Bill Gates "smart and casual" look (or so he says), 20 percent off at Marshall's. Then there's the burgundy striped ties he got at the Burlington Coat Factory—five ties for the price of three. Now that's the stuff. These I wear with the Burberry cufflinks (purchased from Syms) and the Oxford dress shoes (purchased from Payless), 60 percent off original retail price if you buy them between August and September for their Back to School specials. It took a while to figure out how to get the wooden shoe trees back in the shoes after wearing them, but now I'm a pro—I just slip them out and slip his oxfords right on. The space around my toes is really something. I step outside the closet with big, slow strides so the shoes don't slip off mid-step, and I look in the mirror.

I'd like to say I'm reminiscent of a young Denzel Washington or a *Pulp Fiction*-style Samuel L. Jackson right now. But something's not quite right. I open the left mirror cabinet: Tylenol, Benadryl (for sleeping), Lipitor (for high cholesterol, which runs in my family), extra floss, and Vaseline. Behind all this I find the shaving cream—the Taylor of Old Bond Street kind. I know how to beat it real fast so it lathers right up into foam and looks like whipped cream from when he used to let me do this last step for him. Then he'd finish the shave himself with a razor.

Now when it comes time for me to do my face, I put a butter knife to my cheek to wipe off the cream. After a while the cream slides slowly off my face and onto Daddy's shirt, which I then have to wash before Mom finds out. I mean she probably won't, since she's been hiding out in the baby's room all night and day so as not to have to sleep alone in theirs, but still. Afterwards I use the set of grocery bags I have stashed by the mirror to dispose of the evidence. I throw the bag out on the corner when I'm running errands for Mom who's *tired of having to carry the whole household while we just sit there not lifting a finger.* It's OK because that way I can replace the tub of shaving cream before anyone can notice. Still, holding the butter knife smeared with the Taylor of Old Bond Street shaving cream, something's not right.

Like for starters my plaits are too long and wiry-looking. I used to undo them every chance I got, but Mom likes to fuss too much. Secondly, my face is too small. Too bony. My chin looks like the letter V. My eyelashes are long like I took a curler to them—like I'm *trying* to look like a girl. It's embarrassing. My bee stings are turning into giant plums that plop around in front of me wherever I go. It's like some guy decided it would be funny to weld a kick me sign to my chest. I bend my knees so that I can only see myself from the neck up. This helps sometimes.

Dad used to come home from work late to find me in his wardrobe fast asleep under the cardigans we got him for Father's Day last year from JCPenney. He used to pull me out of his closet, put me on his lap and say, "I thought I sensed my shadow in here." But not anymore. The last time he found me like that was right before he left for "Europe." He had this look on his face:

"Don't you have homework?" he asked, eyebrows all raised, lips curled into a doughnut twist.

"Didn't we just give you your own room with an extra egg crate foam mattress last summer? Maybe Zora would be more appreciative," Mom said when he told her later.

"You can call me Ashes," I say in the mirror. It's the name I gave myself. Actually, my new friend Shay gave it to me. "Sound deadly, don't it?" I say with a lower and (in my mind) more debonair voice.

Later on 9/21/1999

So there's this thing that happened in Dad's office two days ago. I don't wanna talk about it. Well, maybe I do. I'm admiring my clean shave in the mirror and feeling kind of pleased with myself when I look in the toilet bowl. It's awful: horrible, evil, red blotches are desecrating the white bowl. It's hard to say whether my mother will be excited for me or whether she'll strap me down and lock me up for becoming a "woman."

Not that I'm going to tell her. I'm not one of those girls who's trying to cheat puberty either. I'm not like Shay. When she takes a shower, she wraps the towel around her waist instead of her chest. I think that's weird. I would never wanna be a boy, but I don't know that I'd ever want to be a woman either. Boys just want to pound each other to the ground and laugh every time they hear a fart or the word *boob* and girls think that's funny. That almost makes girls even worse. Like the other day we were all sitting around in the park and Crystal asked Joey who he thought out of all us girls would give the best head. Joey said Vicky would 'cus she can put a rubber band on a pickle with just her tongue. She was the only girl who could do it when we all tried last summer. But then Jerry said, no, Sasha would, 'cus she got those big black-girl lips. I wanted to knock him into next Tuesday, but I played it cool and said his dick was probably so small it'd be like sucking on a toothpick. Shay gave him a nasty look, but she didn't really say anything to defend me.

9/22/1999: On the Curse of the Red Clap

All the other girls are talking about how they got their periods and when and shit. Nobody can believe that I'm turning fifteen soon and only just got mine. The only person who doesn't sound too excited is Shay. She refers to it as the Red Clap. I remember Mom told me once that your period can be your privilege or your sentence so you'd better use it wisely. Definitely not telling her. Kind of been a pain lying to her though. I've been using my lunch money to buy the pads and I gotta throw them out with the shaving cream. Plus, the cramping's been real bad, but she keeps getting on my case about helping out more before the baby comes and I don't want her to know, so I just put some rice in a sock with a rubber band and microwave it and keep it underneath my belt to help ease the pain.

9/25/1999: Even More on the Curse of the Red Clap

So Mom finally finds out that I've been lying to her about getting my period. And get this: the week I get the Red Clap just so happens to be the week of the annual Back to School potluck. You think this shit's too ironic to be true? Well, fuck, so do I, but it happened.

Right when we're at the school's entrance and trying to get inside, she goes, "I know." She's gripping onto my jacket sleeve pretty hard and I'm not sure what's coming next. I think she's probably about to slap me, but instead she says, "It's beautiful," and she kisses me on the forehead. I'm confused, but I try to smile 'cus I think I must be in the clear—like maybe my mom's a changed woman and this is all that's gonna happen to me tonight. That was until she says something to Mrs. Harpy—mother of Kimberly Harpy and president of the PTA—the one Mom calls Demon Harpie behind her back.

I'm sitting down about to enjoy some macaroni salad and string beans when Harpy taps her glass and announces that Mrs. Porter (my mother) would like to make a toast:

"Ladies and gentleman!" my mother begins in the voice she uses for white people—overly enunciated words with long pauses, like maybe she thinks the stretching out of every vowel will thin out her accent, "My daughter" pause "has recently," tears well up in her eyes, "become a woman!" wipes tears. It's quite the performance, but the smirk out of the corner of her lips lets me know that this was her revenge plan all along and I have to say I'm impressed by how well the punishment fits the crime.

Shit was particularly bad because Shay was sitting two tables away with her eyes turned downward. And when Shay's too embarrassed to even look at you, you know you're never gonna live this one down any time soon with the other kids at school. Of course she might've just had her head down because her grandmother made her wear that girly red sundress. She kept twitching and kicking her legs like that would change something. Though I had to admit that I kinda liked the way her legs looked sturdy underneath her dress. I was trying not to stare at the way she kept flexing her calf muscles as she kicked her legs back and forth, back and forth until her grandmother reprimanded her.

09/28/1999

I walk through the ravine a lot now to clear my head. I think about shit like my Mom and why she didn't just have an abortion. I know I'd never have a baby if my husband was off screwing some young Euro-trash ho in Germany or wherever the fuck he really is. Zora still acts like this shit's not happening, but she wasn't there when the bitch called and I answered the house phone. Dad had already answered from his office line upstairs, so I hung up and picked up again real slow, putting my hand over my nose so they couldn't hear me breathing. Dad was sweet-talking his woman in his half English/half German tongue—sorta like what he used to do with Mom but without the German.

Of course it turned out that he heard me anyway. I figured that out the next morning when he knocked me across my face and slammed me up against my desk. Then I was late to school 'cus I had to ice my cheeks so as not to get those funny looks at school or get sent to the school social worker again.

Anyway, Zora doesn't get that the man's probably been two-timing Mom since before we were born. I'm always worried that even if Zora did know the whole truth—like if I took her aside and told her everything like I used to—that she'd still wind up taking his side and leave me alone to clean up his mess with Mom while the two of them went traveling the world telling stories together.

I can tell stories. Like just last week I told Mom I joined the basketball team, so that I could hang out with the girls in the park. Mom doesn't believe in curfew. She clocked forty-five minutes for the amount of time it should take me to get home. So if I'm home more than fifty minutes after school lets out without an official note from the teacher, I get the switch. But it's worth it. This way I get to hang out with Shay and the others. I met Shay in the park a couple months ago. She's a few grades above me at Erasmus, so we never talked until that day, but I did notice her walking past my locker once dressed like Salt from Salt-N-Pepa. Shit was fly. She even gave me the head nod when she caught me looking. She's kind of a Boss. The coolest girl I know. First time she invited me to sit with her crew, the girls were sitting on the stones in the miniature waterfall drinking bottles of Busch Lights—like it was their own backyard. I was going to keep walking like I didn't even see them, but the girl with earrings that reached her armpits said, "Hey flaca!" and I said, "What?" and another said, "It means you're skinny." This came from the hefty girl with tattoos on her ankles.

"We all bet Shay five beers she can't open this one with her teeth," the first girl said.

"Sure I can," Shay said and smiled, "Learned how from my cousins in Ghana."

"Prove it!" long earrings said.

"OK." Shay took off her hat. Her canerows were large that day. They ran across her whole head, ending just where the neck begins like a boy's. She threw her head back dramatically and lifted the bottle to her mouth. Her teeth cranked away and I was a little worried, but then she had the cap off in seconds—SECONDS!

"Ta-da!" And then she took a bow.

Just when I was starting to like her, she held out her hand and said, "So where's my money? It's five bucks or five beers and I know you ain't got any beer."

I laughed nervously at first.

"No, seriously, where is it?" She took off her black fingerless gloves like she was Madonna or something and started to pat me down. Her fingers touched my bellybutton and I flinched.

"What are you, a cop?" I said, wanting to sound tough. I slapped her hand away when she got closer to my two growing plums—just for emphasis.

"Take it easy," she said, "I'm kidding!" and she slid her fingers into my front pocket, making me jump, and pulled out my wallet. She examined it: my Hello Kitty wallet of shame that I'd been meaning to replace with a cool leather trifold once I could afford one.

"I like her," she said to her crew and they laughed. She handed the wallet back to me.

"Have a beer," long earrings said. "I'm Nina," she said and extended the beer toward me as an introductory gesture.

"Thanks," I said. Truth be told, I was scared, but I stayed anyway. Didn't wanna be called a wuss or nothing. Shay's overall straps were hanging over her waist and through her black-and-yellow skate tee, I could see no plums. I tried not to stare. I was pretty sure she was a girl on account of her voice being girly and the fact that she was dressed like Salt from Salt-N-Pepa the other day.

"So what's your name?" she asked.

"Sasha."

"Sasha," Shay repeated, eyeing me up and down, "We're like two giraffes," she said, because we were both tall and made of bones. I had to smile at that.

10/1/1999: About the Two Giraffes

I think Shay and I are becoming real friends now—even though she's about three years older than me. Once in a while she'll leave her crew to walk me home and invite me to eat ice cream with her and her grandmother. Her grandmother's from Ghana and whenever I see her she gives me a FanIce ice cream pack and I give her a new HitsClip so that she can stay current *with all the racket the kids are listening to these days.* Her grandmother told me about all the words both Jamaican and Trinidadian patois share with her language, Twi. Like *Unnu* or *unu* is the plural word for "you" as in, *what unu pickney doing sittin' pon de television while dishes stay rot in de sink?* And *buller* or *bulla* for penis, sex, and faggot, as in, *a bullet in a bulla go a long way*. Once her grandmother told me that the Anansi stories me and Zora love so much are from Africa and that their Anansi is a selfish, greedy womanizer and not the hero we make him out to be. This shocked me quite a bit. When I asked Mom, she called her a liar, but I didn't see how a woman with so many wrinkles could lie like that.

10/3/1999: On How I Discovered Plum Wrapping

The first time we're in her room she locks the door and pulls me onto her bed.

"I know you're curious," she says and I wonder if we're gonna kiss. I don't know if I feel excited or sick to my stomach that she would even dare. Her breath smells like Bubble Tape. Her eyes are mischievous slits. She takes off her T-shirt. It's the first half naked body I've ever seen besides my sister's. Her plums are being flattened by Ace bandage wrap and held together with masking tape. She smiles when she sees me looking at her chest and tries to take my hand, but I snatch it away. Suddenly I'm not sure I'm up for the challenge.

Shay throws her head back and laughs, "You can touch it," she says, "They don't bite." I look into my hands nervously. I was hoping for a bit more romance before this stage.

"Don't worry, Abus," she says. She always brings in her Twi dialect, which makes me shameful 'cus I never learned to speak patois from my parents, only to understand it. "I only date femmes." She can tell from my shrug that I have no idea what she's talking about. She continues, "Girly girls. Not butches like me and you."

My chest tightens when she says that. I look away, trying to focus on the floral pattern on her bed, the swirls making my head hurt.

"Look, I only brought you in here 'cus I thought you'd maybe wanna try. Wrapping, I mean. I could show you."

"What makes you think I'd wanna try that?"

Actually, I do know why. It's 'cus of the time we were all talking about who had the nicest plums (she calls them titties) and I said that she did because you could hardly see them. I said I liked the way her torso looked sturdy and fit like a man's. The other girls laughed and two of them were whispering something that I'm sure was about me, but I just shrugged them off. But still, I didn't like the way she was being so crude about it, *butches like you*. Shit. I mean yeah I think she's cool and I like the way she dresses and stuff. But that doesn't mean nothing. Just because I wear my dad's clothes sometimes and just because I never had a boyfriend. Lord knows Zora never did. True, I was annoyed that Zora got kissed before I did. But it's not like I have too many crushes. I'm just picky that's all. And it's not like we're really allowed to talk to boys anyway.

"Look, just because I said that I'd like to be smaller up here" (I'm pointing to my plums), "Doesn't mean that I'm like…"

"A dyke?" She sighs, puts her shirt back on, puts her hands on her knees and stares me down, cold, "My father hates them too, you know."

Her emphasis on the word *too* causes me to wrap my hand around my stomach and start to feel nauseous.

"My mom's probably wondering why I'm not home for dinner. I should probably go," I say. But as soon as I get home, there I am in the mirror: upset at the sight of those plums—embarrassing hanging plums that hurt when I do jumping jacks in gym class. I wonder if she's right about what she said. *Butches like you.* So the next day in school I say, "OK." She smiles and says, "Friday."

Shay tapes her two plums down with tape every morning in the bathroom of McDonalds before school starts. She has to untape them before her grandma gets home from volunteering at her church at 5 pm. Shay taught me that if you take the pill each month a week or two before you're supposed to get your period that you can stop getting it forever. "Worst day of my life," she said, "Looked in the toilet and thought I would die."

I smile in recognition. She doesn't bring up the potluck, but I can tell that this is her way of saying she understands what I'm going through.

She smiles and then: "OK, are you ready now? You're going to have to take off your shirt."

"All right." I breathe deep. "But, no peeking." I take it off. She unrolls the Ace bandage slowly. She holds my arms out and my body jumps a little as she circles around me with the wrap, her fingers pressing into me, reaching across my plums for a split second. I don't like to admit it, but I'm disappointed she didn't stay there longer. She gives me a Hilfiger button-down and some jeans to try on.

"You look good," she says.

I smile.

"So, what're you doing this Friday?"

I shrug.

"The Bulldogs are having a party to celebrate making it into the play-offs. You should come."

"You sure we can get into that? I mean, isn't that a college party?"

"Don't be a wuss, Sasha. You'll never get laid."

She had me there.

"Butches gotta be fierce. In fact, I got a new nickname for you: Ashes. Sound deadly, don't it?"

Shay's real name is Shyanne, but only her grandma calls her that. Her mother's a nurse and her father works on AIDS policy in government. He went back to Ghana to do some diplomacy shit, blames the gays for everything, sent her to her grandma to be raised with Ghanaian (Christian) values.

"So how come you only date girly girls?" I ask. I'm thinking about the time where we were first starting to hang out. Nina had said that Taylor—the boy with the washed-out Nikes wanted to talk to me after school on Friday and I said I didn't know if I could go out with someone who spelled believable B-E-L-E-V-I-B-L-E. Nina laughed, but Shay asked me later, "So, are you talking to him or what?" Eyes hardly blinked or nothing. I shook my head, "Hell no," and she said, "Good" with a smile that looked like more than friendship.

"Look, you better come to the party, Ashes. You can even bring your sister," she says, not answering my previous question. She writes down the address for me and places it in my hand. She leaves her fingers in my palm longer than she needs to—or that's what it feels like. A part of me wants to move my hand away, but I don't.

Later on 10/3/1999

I get home and Zora's yelling, "Where have you been?" and shit like that the second I walk through the door.

"Yeah yeah yeah," I say, walking past her into my room and slamming the door. I can't handle her. Not now.

Of course a few moments later there she is lurking in my doorway, holding an envelope. She comes and sits on my bed. "Sasha?" she asks.

"Zora, can't you see that I'm not in the mood?"

"It's just…you seem so mad lately. And you're never around."

I can see she needs some kind of reassurance from me that shows that things are still OK, so I say, "You know that girl Shay from my school? You hung out with us once at her grandma's house?"

"The one who dresses like a man?"

"Yeah, Zora. That one. What do you think about her? Like, what if I dressed like that?"

"Like a hooligan?"

"See, Zora, this is exactly why I can't tell you things."

"No, Sasha, you got to," she says, almost pleading. "Look, you were right," she says and hands me the envelope in her hand. It's addressed to our father. It has no return address, but it was probably sent internationally based on the postage.

"It was in the trash. Can you believe it? That she would write a letter. HERE?"

"What? Let me see that," I say, grabbing the envelope so I can see it properly. I run my hands over the envelope.

"So what do you think?"

I shrug. "Figures, I guess."

"Well, I still can't believe it. I was waiting for you to open it…so should we?"

"I don't know, I'm thinking. Maybe there's things you're better off not knowing."

"What's that supposed to mean?"

"I dunno…Look, can't we talk about this later? I got a lot of studying to do for Ms. Blight's test tomorrow if I wanna keep Mom and Dad off my back."

The other thing I should probably tell you is that there is in fact another thing that happened. Just a few days ago. I can't seem to get this one out of my head. I was walking out of the park using the Grand Army Plaza exit when I saw someone who had to be my father getting out of a car on Prospect Park West and entering an apartment building. One of those buildings where white people like psychiatrists and occupational therapists with home offices live. Dad was wearing the Gray Crew Neck with khakis and sunglasses. That was all I could see.

10/8/1999: So I Decide to Tell Zora

"I saw Dad," I tell her.

She moves closer to me and puts her hand on my arm, "Where'd you see him?"

"Prospect Park West and Seventh. Close to the Bandshell."

"When?"

"Few days ago."

She nods.

"Was he with anyone?"

"I don't know."

The conversation doesn't go much further. We watch *The Shining* to get our mind off things. Mom cooks Pelau for the third time in a row.

The next day, after school, she says "Let's go find him." And so we stand by the building: number 3010 on Seventh and Prospect Park West. I even ask the doorman, giving him the name Adaliz Austerlitz while Zora waits outside.

"We don't give out tenant information," he says and escorts me back to the exit.

10/10/1999

I start walking down Prospect Park West every day after school to see if I can find him. When I don't, I think about Shay instead, the feel of her calf muscles if they were next to mine.

10/11/1999

Today Mom found out that I'm not really on the girls basketball team so now I'm in some real shit. Also, she says Dad's coming home. She claims he'll be back before her due date, which is in less than two weeks. I can't tell if she's for real or not.

10/12/1999

She's for real. She made us clean the walls with vinegar this time. She even bought some chicken to jerk, which just so happens to be Dad's favorite. Maybe I never saw him in the park after all.

10/13/1999: The Night of the Party

Is when we decide to make the plan of all plans: me and Zora are pretending that we're staying over at Kelly's—the Christian girl with all the cats whose grandmother loves our mother and vice versa. See Kelly's been owing Zora this favor ever since Zora let Kelly copy her Spanish homework for like a week when she was out with the flu and didn't feel like making it all up in one go. Now in exchange for this favor, I gotta take on all of Zora's chores until the baby comes, but that's pretty much a walk in the park for me, since I'm basically grounded anyway, except for tonight. Still, it's cool that Zora's helping me to get ready for the party even though I told her that she's too young to come with me 'cus I don't want her to embarrass me and all that. She even helped me pick out my entire outfit. She put a doo-rag over my head and had me choose the pinstriped button-down from Dad's closet instead of the horizontal stripes I was initially going to go with. Girl has taste.

When we finish, Zora stands before me, admiring her creation.

"Well, you did it," she says. "You look just like a man." She was also being nice to make up for calling Shay a hooligan the other day. Had to give her credit for that.

"Yeah, but what kind of man? I mean do I look like Denzel or what?"

"I wouldn't go that far."

"Samuel L. Jackson?"

"I don't know about all that, Sasha. Maybe like Marlon Wayans. Maybe," and then, "So you like her, don't ya? Shay, I mean."

I roll my eyes in response.

"It's OK. I mean if you're going to Hell, then so am I." She smiles. I had to smile back at her for that.

"The thing is, we're cool 'cus we both like to dress all butch or whatever—you know, all masculine-like?"

Nods.

"But, she says she only dates girly girls."

"Sounds like a conundrum."

"Well, yeah."

"Maybe dress like a girl for a night, get her all excited and then say, see it's the inside that counts."

"That's corny, Zora."

"I dunno, maybe she likes that gushy stuff. I know I would."

"You and me are different, Zora. You think you're going to Hell every time you use a four-letter word. The only sinful thoughts you have are watching Rated R movies and setting imaginary hexes on Mrs. Bolax."

Zora had the look like she was going to say something, but she just got quiet instead.

10/14/1999: The Aftermath: Where Shit Really Hits the Fan

The party was all right. Shay spent the whole time talking to this fucking cheerleader with braces.

"Yo, white girls are so easy," she told me later. "All it took was for her boyfriend to leave and a double shot of Malibu and she was ALL over me." We were standing alone out on the curb while she smoked a cigarette. She tried to give me the pound, but I just rolled my eyes and shifted away from her.

"She's probably just using you." I tried to sound real casual and looked out at the cars so she couldn't read my face.

"Oh don't be mad just 'cus you ain't got game, sis. You just wanna sit in the corner and wait for the girls to come to you. Femmes expect butches to be like men—only nicer. We gotta make the first move."

"Don't call me Sis."

"Whatever."

I left early even though the plan was to spend the whole night out so as not to ruin our whole alibi. I could've gone to Kelly's, but I didn't wanna have to deal with Zora asking me how it went and all that.

So I went home. I came in through the kitchen entrance and there he was standing in the kitchen with a glass of whiskey in hand.

"Daddy?" I got closer, wanting to poke him to make sure he was real.

"Sasha," he says. His voice was tired.

A part of me wanted to hug him, but I didn't.

"Would you like to explain to me what you're doing walking in at this hour?"

"Nothing…I mean I was over at Kelly's house with Zora, but I felt sick, so I came home."

And that's when he looked me up and down assessing the button-down I took from his closet, the Birkenstock knock-offs, the Hilfiger jeans I borrowed from Shay the day before. I shielded my face just in case a slap was coming or something worse.

"It's nice to see you, Sasha. We'll talk about this tomorrow," he said, "Go upstairs and get to bed before your mother hears you. It's a school night."

10/15/1999: Dad's Home

Like nothing's changed. Mom seems happy he's here, but quieter too. His first day back and it's like they've stopped fighting altogether. Of course they don't really talk much either. If he walks in the kitchen, she leaves to use the restroom. If she's lying on the sofa watching *Matlock* or getting Zora to rub her belly, Dad goes out for a walk or he goes to get something or other from the store. I'm glad because it means he probably hasn't had the chance to tell her about me coming in late last night, dressed like a man. I wanna say things like, where the fuck have you been, but he's the first to speak:

"Let's go for a walk," he says. We walk through the park the way we used to and I feel lucky that he took me and not Zora, like maybe I can be his favorite too. Of course, I also feel pretty tense, knowing that he could snap at me at any moment, call me a mannish girl or a sodomite or worse. As we walk, he points out the technical names for flowers, saying things like, "These are known as the prunus serrulata. Sakura in Japanese," and, "It's too bad the Cherry Blossom festival is over and done with at the gardens this year. I would've loved to take you there." His voice has this new zest to it. I try to listen out for that turn to the sharper tone, the one where he emphasizes all the consonants—something to signal that things are about to change so that I'll expect it before he throws me to the ground and casts me out from the entire family.

We exit at Grand Army Plaza and I know that it's happening. We take the elevator to the Eighteenth floor. Inside the apartment, the AC is on high and it smells of too much air freshener, kitty litter, and dog hair. But there's also a real hardwood floor (instead of carpet) and a real marble counter. Also, the expensive looking couches don't have the plastic covering over them the way that ours do. There is a real porcelain bowl with real fruit to eat and candles that have been taken out of the wrapper. And there are dogs. Certainly not a Caribbean household. I look at everything in the house before I look at her.

"Aren't you going to say something?" my father asks me in his trying to be polite around whitefolks voice.

"Oh, it's nice to meet you, Mrs..."

"Call me Aunty Adeliz," the woman says. She holds out her hand with painted fingernails. She's wearing a large red cashmere sweater and khaki slacks. She has long blond hair that reaches to the middle of her back. Not nearly as pretty as Mom. She isn't even all that skinny. Probably makes good money, though, from the looks of things. She asks me if I want any chocolates. She says she brought them all the way from Germany. I say nothing, but Dad says, "Of course she does," and stuffs some in my palms. The woman looks real nervous suddenly, shuffling back and forth, rubbing her hand around her stomach in slow meditative motions. It takes me a minute of staring at her hand-over-stomach to realize that she's rubbing what looks a lot like Mom's belly bump a few months in.

"How long has she been living there?" I ask when we leave.

"Don't tell your mother about this," he says instead, "She's just an old friend I like to visit from time to time."

"Oh, so why'd you want me to meet her then?"

"She's an important contact for you to have. Graduated third in her class from Oxford. You need to start thinking more seriously about your future at your age. Needless to say that nobody is impressed with your academic performance of late."

"Oh. Right. OK," I sort of mumble.

"Speak up, Sasha. Speak like a lady."

"Thank-you, Daddy," I say instead.

"You're welcome. And don't repeat any of this to Zora. She's too young to understand."

"About going to college?"

"Don't be smart, Sasha."

Yep, things are getting back to normal all right.

10/18/1999

Since that day, I've started finding new ways to sneak out of the house. Sometimes one of them will catch me and I'll get the switch, but that's about as bad as it gets, and it probably would've happened anyway based on how I've been doing in school. My progress reports will come through the mail any day now. Not only am I already failing math, but I'm also failing chem., US History, and only pulling a C+ in British Lit. Dad hasn't really been on my back, 'cus of the deal I guess we made. The one where I say nothing and he and Mom hold off on giving me the switch or the belt or the swizzle stick for a while. Turns out the reason he knew about me is that doorman. I guess he doesn't know that Zora was there too, since I was the one who actually went inside the building and asked the man for Adaliz Austerlitz's apartment number. Zora's not sure if we should tell Mom about what happened. Yeah, I told Zora eventually.

10/21/1999: My Last Entry for a While

At some point I decide to tell Mom. I run all the way home, ready to tell her everything. Like maybe if she knew this time she'd leave him for good. But I get inside and there *he* is, holding *my* baby sister. Mom's standing right beside him with a sleepy grin on her face. Georgia, the doula, and

Annie, the midwife, are sitting on the sofa holding some paperwork. Zora's there too, gazing in amazement like this child's the second coming or something. If you ask me, she's the ugliest baby I've ever seen: bald and wet-looking bundle with eyes and puny alien-looking limbs.

"Come give your new sister a kiss," Mom says.

"Don't you want to hold your sister?" Dad asks.

I wanna say no, but my tongue feels frozen, so I just stare at the thing. With all the crowding around it and with Zora poking at it like it's pudding, I decide to stay put. Another sister. Lucky me.

"You've got to be fucking kidding me," I say. I storm into my room before either one of them can run after me with the swizzle stick. I lie on my bed for a minute, then two. Nobody comes. "Well, shit, maybe now they'll finally treat me like the fucking older sister for once. Can say whatever the fuck I want." Nobody hears me.

Eventually I get hungry, so I have to go outside. In the living room, Zora's holding the baby and making stupid faces. Mom is on the couch looking zonked out of her mind. And Dad? He's on the floor, her feet in his hands. He looks up at me and puts a finger to his lips. "Your mother needs her rest," he whispers. I walk tentatively toward the family huddle, confused. "Things aren't going back to normal," I say.

"No, they're not," he agrees. He motions for me to sit by him. His Polo button-down looks looser than usual. His broad arms look flabbier, more tired.

He strains a smile. "How about I let you two take over," he says to Zora and me before walking into his room and closing the door.

"You ready to hold her yet?" Zora asks me when he leaves.

I look at Zora hesitantly and then at the alien. I wonder how long it will be till Dad sneaks off to his other baby—the whiter one. I wonder how long it will take him to leave us altogether.

"All right," I say anyway and attempt to hold her. The baby feels less alien-like now that she's in my arms. She opens her mouth into an O, yawning, stretching bony stick fingers out to me.

"She's cute," I say.

"Things will be different now, Sasha. You'll see." She has this wise older sister look on her face that I've never seen her wear before.

I look at her incredulously. "If you say so, Zora."

After a few minutes of me holding the baby, Mom starts to stretch and opens her eyes. She smiles at us being sisterly toward one another.

"Look who's returned," Mom says, pointing a lazy finger at me.

She looks pretty worn, but there's still a grin on her face. I look from the baby to Mom, deciding if I should just say it when Zora steps in, stealing my thunder: "Dad's cheating again. This time it's serious."

"Zora!" I say. I can't decide if I'm mad that she beat me to the punch or if I'm suddenly thinking that telling Mom is a bad idea.

Mom just shifts, then yawns. Says nothing.

Zora keeps going, "We think he got her pregnant. And there's letters."

Mom laughs a girl's giggle that transforms into a woman's cackle. "So I see him twenty-woman-a-week lifestyle finally catch up wid him, eh," she says, still laughing. "Steups," she sucks her teeth, "Just hush chile and let me see my baby girl."

I bring my new sister toward her. She takes her from me, stroking her face and head.

"A mistress with child is a whole new game. Maybe now he'll learn," she says.

"Aren't you even mad at him?" Zora asks.

I don't say anything, but of course I'm wondering the same thing.

"More important things on my mind," she says, "You might understand it one day."

We look at her, both concerned. She reaches her free hand toward us, beckoning. "Then again, I hope you won't," she says and smiles. She goes back to ogling over her baby girl.

I can't figure out if it's the baby or the fact that Zora's news holds some kind of redemptive power over Mom—freeing her from worrying about what she's always known to be true, but the woman looks positively giddy. Things will be different all right. I just can't tell if this'll be a good different or a bad different quite yet. Still, if you were just watching us all huddled around the baby with sleepy grins and didn't know our story, you could take a picture, put us on the front cover of *National Geographic*, call us, "The new mosaic American family"—the perfect Kodak moment.

PATRICK PHILLIPS
The Diarist

It's one long list
of births and deaths,

baptisms and christenings,
and who married whom,

and where, and when—
all fading into

the ornate script
of a century so distant

it seems less lived
than this one—

until I reach *Novembre,*
Sixteen Forty Five,

where she left no trace
for nineteen days,

then: *Peter, a son.*
He did not thrive.

Body Knowledge

Pragmatic heeding
Of the majority host, in
Religions or tongues:
The deaf children jabber
In Sign, then they subside
At their teacher's gesture
For quiet: one finger to her lip.

Acceding for survival is
Second nature. A passage
Of music mastered is burnt
Into the brain—a fact I
Accepted even though
In actual music I felt it
Inside my fingers,
A fluency as intimate
And assured as gestures
Of insult, the Bird, the Fig.
In Italy if my knuckles
Brush my chin backhand
Toward you, it's: I hereby
Disrespect you, I pull
Your beard, face to face.

Or nearly the opposite: my soul
Sweating to get something
Right in this, the tragic
Chorus: our singular "I"
In plural unison, chanting
And miming our civic agony,
The hero with his second nature
Ardently at war with the first.

STANLEY PLUMLY
Poliomyelitis

Magical numbers! Roosevelt the most famous infantile paralysis
adult to ever live with it, thrive with it, die with it, at sixty-three,
contracted at thirty-nine, the same integral number as my birth year
and the year, 1939, when the world war that changes everything starts—
the President treading water with his hands and arms, standing
at poolside in Warm Springs, the life in his legs different from any feeling.
Polio the proof that the child in us never disappears but turns against us
just when we think we've outgrown its memory and become who we are
and were meant to be, a whole other human body with a mind like a city,
more beautiful at night, while the still heart is a pastoral, with a piper.
A man said Roosevelt, at the end, looked like the most dead man alive
he'd ever seen: the girl in the iron lung, too, resembling what children
imagine death in the satin of its coffin looks like, her face roughed up
with rouge, her soft brown hair straightened, the rest of her forgotten.

ROBERT POLITO
Love in Vain

Of our first album critics remember
only the flaws. Major domo/manager/producer,

I recorded the band live from Boston's Park St. Station—

over a pay phone to my parents' house in Quincy.
Rush-hour subway screech tilting everything apocalyptic,
amid the operator's recurrent

ten cents for three more minutes, please.

"I had nothing to lose," Molloy said, "I would have made love
with a goat, to know what love was."

Our repertoire a mangle of Peking Opera gong & folk blues
turning on toxic mishearing of the plaints.
It's hard to tell, hard to tell

(as *ka-ching!* another dime drops)

hard to tell when all your blood's in Maine.

PAISLEY REKDAL
Astyanax

They laughed, at first, at his shrieks
seeing the face his father wore: a horse head
mask unearthed from the closet
where he kept his army uniform, the white
rubber face with real hair for a mane
under which his father's shoulders bulged.
His father's large hands tossed the boy
into the air then onto his back, bucking him
across the carpet. He clung to him, this boy
who had never before seen an animal
like his father, though they read him stories
of ponies and gentle cart horses, bulls
in a field eating flowers, once a bugling buck
with its brace of horns.
Nothing like this. The teacup nostrils
flamed with blood, the pink lips cracked back
into a sneer. It filled the air
with muffled cries, its long mane dark
as his mother's hair, and just as fine, as if
he'd shorn it from her: this thing
racing now to the kitchen where
it would kick the whole
house down, jump the fence, tear
off with him across oceans.
The white skin sagged at the neck.
Perhaps, if they took this face off, his father
would return and he could stop crying,
though when the mask came off
the boy did not stop crying: there were
powdery creases now in his father's face,
and his skin smelled bitter, burning.
His father tossed the mask aside
and pressed his son's face into his neck.

And still the boy did not stop crying, could not stop
seeing this wild, gray face even in sleep, and so woke
crying again the next morning, regardless
of his mother's songs, his father's smiles;
regardless of how his parents tried
to make a joke of it. How they laughed
and laughed, who loved him
and could not console him.

MAURICE RIORDAN
Feet

We were sitting in the restaurant window
when I heard myself saying *Seamus is here*–
though there was no greeting, and our view was blocked
by a brewery lorry pulled up on the kerb.
I'd no sight of him, but it was nothing spooky either.
What I had seen under the lorry were two feet
passing on the other side. I'd known him by the gait,
as one would by the voice. Yet I'd never before
noticed his feet—and, if asked, I might have guessed
he had a fisherman's walk, slow and deliberate.
But no, what I saw were the feet of a schoolboy
invisibly sandaled, stepping nimbly toward us.

DAVID RIVARD
That Year

I meet Margaret Mead that year—
"that old lady,
what a pain in the ass she is!"—
or so her helper says,
a dreadlocked Dominican from Yonkers;
but outside her suite
at the Museum of Natural History
in the corner turret high above 77th & Columbus
after she's pottered off
I take photos of the shadow puppets
she'd collected in Bali
alongside Bateson, her ex-husband Gregory
Bateson—he'd divorced her & moved on
to cybernetics & the study of
dolphin speech, the mammal chatter
he'd reported
hearing in Caribbean waters
as feedback, coded & algorithmic—
life was a construction of encoded systems,
my teachers claimed—
the epic stories these puppets played out
in the *wayang kulit*, each propped for an eternity
or two against a white sheet,
the bejeweled warriors & courtesans
killer gods and goddesses
Ganesh, the Remover of Obstacles
Rama, Sita, Hanuman, Arjuna,
the projected lives of all
the monkey lords & cloud dwellers—
my life near Exit 8 off the Jersey Pike
next door to Jim & Cyndi,
friendly potheads & printer's devils—
1976—my shantytown year in New Jersey

at the graduate school of anthropology—
a rake's progress already in progress there
each week
as I deal pot & acid to moneyed undergrads
in the eating clubs at Princeton
all the while
reading Lacan & Lévi-Strauss,
a kinship economy of the sort
referred to in passing by Clifford Geertz
when he lectures in March
at the Institute for Advanced Study—
he quoted Olson then:
"The first fact of America is space,"
a fact so obvious
its implications were made impossible
to prove either true or false—
my teachers were wrong—
there is no code,
no use for the beautiful
and ornate key they pressed so
eagerly into my hands.

My Mother Addresses Everyone in the World

So you think I couldn't have been the life
of your miserable party.

You think because I graded
9th-grade quizzes into the night
I was probably fit for just that.
You think I didn't finish my novel
because I feared it might not sell.

You assume because my immigrant parents
refused to teach me their language
I didn't know what they were saying.

You think that having children
was my way of creating the siblings
I never had.

You think it's been easy
pretending to be one of you.

You think I couldn't have made it on Broadway,
that I couldn't have managed your company,
your portfolio, kept the whole country in the black.

You think I devoted my energies
to amateur theater and making root beer
and dandelion wine,
to gardening, canning, baking,
ventriloquism, quilting,
beekeeping, silkscreening,
and candlemaking, in order
to put off projects I deeply cared about
that might have failed.

You think they would have failed.

You think I was happy enough.
You think I had my life coming to me.

May my daughter prove you wrong.

Three Days Flu No Shower

My armpits smell like Campbell's soup
and my hair feels like the welcome mat
beneath the sign to wipe your feet
between the showroom and the shop.

Who's the new guy sweeping up?
Six bucks an hour, off the books.
Outside the showroom and the shop,
he sleeps in cabs of junkyard trucks,

eats at the Arco Mini-Mart,
jumbo Skippy and Wonder Bread,
dreams that he's a peanut fart,
awakes amazed he isn't dead.

But now he's at the Sunshine Inn,
eight to a room, sleeping in shifts.
He's got the bed from four to ten
and privileges in the kitchenette.

Between the showroom and the shop,
he leans his push broom and he stops.
Beef Barley soup as it plops
out of the can into a thin tin pot.

LLOYD SCHWARTZ
The Conductor

Breezing easily between exotic Chinoiserie
and hometown hoedown, whisking lightly between
woodwind delicacy and jazzy trombone, he must have
the widest and oddest repertoire of gestures, which
allows him a stylistic and dynamic range unusual
even among today's most highly regarded conductors.
The way he slipped from the grandiose opening Adagio
maestoso to the suddenly jaunty Allegretto made me
laugh out loud. Though his small, complex gesticulations
can diminish and even undermine the passages
where the melodic lines ought to soar.

He's all dippy knees, flappy elbows, and floppy wrists.
Not Bernstein's exaggerated self-immolation, but
little, complicated pantomimes: steering a car down a
winding road, patting down a mud pie, robbing eggs
from a bird's nest (and carrying them carefully away), flinging
tinsel on a Christmas tree.
                            As a baseball umpire, he could
declare a runner simultaneously safe and out at home plate.

He threw himself into the music—and very nearly into
the first violin section—with the kind of reckless abandon
that comes only with complete confidence and authority;
not so much confidence in himself and authority over
his players, but confidence in his players, and authority
over his material.

                    These glittering performances: more
dazzle than warmth, more brilliance than magic. Sophistication

without innocence. Does the music ever hold surprises
even for himself? Or terrors?

How much would we love him if it did?

HELEN SCHULMAN
In a Better Place

We were driving back from a weekend away at a friend's house in Normandy when I thought I saw my father—his pebbly gray ashes indisputably scattered and sunk in the icy Atlantic ten long winters before—now alive and well, a passenger in a neighboring coupe. "Dad," I whispered in astonishment, like a little extra exhalation of breath. It was a word I hadn't uttered with ownership in years; it felt both primal and alien in my mouth.

My husband, at the wheel, swerved upon command when I called out, "Follow that car," as if he, Walker, were a taxi driver and we had just left one world and permeated a thin membrane of light and dark filmstrip into another: an old screwball comedy. Which in retrospect was what I suppose we had actually done, weaving in and out of traffic like that, giddily chasing the dead.

We'd recently moved to Paris, ostensibly for work. Walker had a commission. He'd been asked by the Paris Opera to stage some something; he called it "a dance with voice." (Theater people love to speak simply; it's an inverse pretension). My aged mother—poor thing, paralyzed and demented—had finally died. This loss somehow, even at my age, untethered me from the earth, but also, oddly, set us free. So with our beloved daughter Kate's support and encouragement, we sublet our apartment on the Upper West Side to a little lawyer friend of hers, and in the bubbling murk of Walker's and my collective unspoken truths (aka marriage) we flew, *flew*, from continent to continent across the black void of night, with the concrete surface of the ocean a mere death spiral below. The idea was not only to grab opportunity by its willowy throat but to see if Paris, that chilly, damp, lonely city couldn't elevate my mood.

That is how we found ourselves on the road, stalking a ghost, on a carbo-high from a bag full of croissants, Walker momentarily morphing into one of those nutty European drivers—as he cut people off, he strangely seemed to be smoking and cursing in a Marseillan dialect—when we passed a tractor-trailer on the left and I got a better look in that red Audi. It was my father all right. I knew his nose, prominent and hooked. When the life drained out of him, I'd watched it turn blue. Empty as a shell, his cadaver. I finally saw where he'd gone.

"Stay on his ass, Walker," I said.

Remarkably, he obeyed me.

This little side trip to Normandy had come after several months in Europe. An old producer of mine, from the L.A. days when I dabbled in screenplays, Harry Epstein, a chatty guy, a good egg, a rich good egg, had heard through the grapevine that we were in France and called to ask if we'd like to spend a weekend at his home in Normandy. They'd have to sell it off soon, Harry said, he and his third wife, Chang, too expensive and self-indulgent a party prop in these hard times to keep, but it was sitting empty and he thought it might be just the thing… Harry said this last clause with an ellipsis. He had a heart, and a soft spot for the thing I do: spinning my life round and round in a blender and seeing what's left of it mounted on a stage.

So on a Friday afternoon, Walker and I rented a car and drove from the city, stopping in Giverny to give Monet's gardens a postcollegiate whirl and arriving later at the château than we'd planned. That huge old drafty castle was so crazy beautiful it could have cured anyone of anything. Except, apparently, me. There was a maid to greet us and serve us supper and a cook to cook, which she evidently did—the meat at least—over an open flame. Saturday night, though, we were on our own, and since we'd gone to Bayreux in the morning to see the tapestry and to Mont-Saint-Michel to watch the tide recede and the mud bubble up, we were content to eat at a simple farm restaurant on the way home; that was lovely too, the stone archways and wooden floors, the chicken and the duck, the Calvados and *tarte au pomme*. Had Kate and her wife been with us—there was a delicate omelet vegetarian on the plat du jour—the dinner would have been perfect. We even had good sex that night, then slept apart in the twin beds, under heavy, dark oil paintings and acres of blue toile that drew residual patterns on the inner lids of my closed eyes, but when I woke the next day, I didn't quite know where I was, still confused and misplaced in the world perhaps, though filled with a guilt-ridden gratitude for all the gifts that surrounded us, that for the life of me I just couldn't seem to enjoy.

In the morning, we sipped our coffee at the town bar, standing next to some still-drunk old men with their breakfast tumblers of wine. Then we shopped at the tiny boulangerie next door, buying that aforementioned bag of croissants, the kind that shatter properly when torn, the butter rendering the folded puff pastry into thin yeasty layers of air and glass and grease, and hopped back into our car. We were on our way to see the beaches almost seventy years after they were covered in blood and boys, and long restored to their natural glory, when that little red Audi slid into the other lane. We tailed it in hot pursuit for a few minutes, but the traffic was so intense and full of like-hued cars we lost him almost as soon as I'd found him. My daddy.

"Who was it?" asked Walker, finally coming up for air—he'd been concentrating on the road that hard. "Can you see them up ahead?"

He was trying to make me happy. His curse. He'd wasted decades of his life this way. Probably he thought I'd spied a friend, or an Al Qaeda henchman, or a famous actor we'd both worked with and still dined out on at industry dinner parties. How could I explain whom I'd actually seen without sounding totally insane? My father had taken a fall one night in 1999 when he'd gotten up to go to the bathroom. Mr. Cardiac Infarction. All that aspirin. Two cerebral hemorrhages, two surgeries. He'd died in my arms, a long process of agonizingly paced stolen breaths, the fluid in his lungs, the ICU nurse suggested, drowning him. It was Walker, then, when I got home that afternoon, out of a stubborn and innate humanitarianism, who had forced me to eat something. It was always poor Walker.

"I thought I saw Brad Pitt," I said. "Sorry, Walky, a wild goose chase."

Still handsome and brilliant, tired of me, beaten-down, green-eyed, silver-haired Walker. He looked at me now with disgust, anguish, pity—and a hint of boredom thrown in. He'd been here before.

"I'll treat you to a *grande plate de fruit de mer*," I said, wanting to make it up to him. A tower of icy seafood.

"Anna," he said. All the sentences in his head came out encapsulated in that one word.

It's my name, Anna. Anna Herrera. I picked up the ethnic surname in a short heartbreak of a marriage, a name that has stood me well all these years, grant- and prize-wise. Miguel, too, has been dead so long now (AIDS) it is sometimes hard to conjure up my first husband's striking face. We had tried to stay together, even though he couldn't stop sleeping with men, because we loved each other. Such young, innocent knuckleheads. What an idiot I was.

Sometimes, Miguel and I would smoke dope and try sex with me on my stomach, my breasts hidden, flattened out, which helped sort of, but not much. That left breast that I worked so hard to hang on to a couple of years ago, I tucked inward, toward my heart.

Later that day, Walker ended up parking in a little public lot in Arromanches, a tiny port town just a few miles down the coast from Omaha beach. We strolled past several war souvenir shops, on our way to the waterfront restaurant Harry had recommended, stopping in one to peruse.

"Check this out," said Walker. "They have Prince Albert in a can." And so they did. Pipe tobacco that gave fodder to practical jokes from our parents' youth. "Got Prince Albert in a can?" "Then let him out." Ha, Ha. Walker was amused. They had к-rations from the war, still packed. "Enough botulism in one of these to freeze the foreheads of all of CAA," Walker said, somewhat bitterly. (Fun fact: Directors abhor Botox. One of the things Walker actually still liked about me is that I have a face that moves.) A pile of helmets and boots. On the wall above the cash register hung a photo of a GI, a Lucky Strike dangling from his smiling lips, being kissed on each cheek sandwich-style by two grateful old French women, one with skin like mine.

"Do you think Kate and Lulu would fancy that as a souvenir?" I pointed to the picture. Kate's wife, Lucinda, is an activist, who looks and dresses like a boy—she even has a little fuzzy blond beard that I have grown quite fond of. Kate also has a job she likes, working in Internet PR, or we would have forced her and Lucinda to come visit already. It was hard to be away from our daughter for long. Kate's field is crisis management; I suppose that after growing up with us, she's come by her talents honestly.

Walker shrugged. "I think we can do better at the flea markets. I saw some translucent opaline glassware there last week that kind of screamed the girls to me. Remember their last dinner party?"

How could I forget it? It had been so elegant. Lucinda cooked a daube for the meat-eaters, Kate made some philo-cheesy thing. They'd seemed so happy, they'd inspired me. It was after that night, in fact, that I booked our flight to France. And so grown up! Kate sporting the diamond stud earrings Lucinda had bought for her on their second anniversary. Black nails, red lips. Kate looking like a piece of candy.

"I'm hungry," he said. "How about some Freedom fries?"

We exited without a purchase and walked down a long alley, past several moules-frites shops, to the water. The restaurant Harry had suggested sat on a boardwalk, directly on top of the sand.

The beach was flat and the color of a Siamese cat, camel and black and brown—the water flat too, a dull pewter. Once upon a time, at low tide, the habit of the surf had been interrupted by brave young men flinging their bodies in front of bullets, willing to save the world.

At the outdoor terrace, Walker asked for a *table a deux*—he speaks French, I speak "menu"—and the maître d' took us to our seats parallel to the sea. As he pulled out my chair and I sat down, I noticed that across and to the left sat a good-looking woman at a neighboring table. She was in her forties, younger than me, African, wearing a long strapless sundress, her bare shoulders round and gleaming. There was a large green leafy pattern with bright orange flowers on the fabric, blossoms open, stamens showing. She shared a tower of fresh seafood on ice with her companion, that same platter I'd promised Walker. Oysters on the half shell, boiled crab, large langoustines, tiny little cockles swimming in brine. She held an oyster out for him to sup and he leaned in and swallowed it whole, pinkening like lobster meat over heat, smitten.

That nose, those skinny hands, piano fingers. It was my father. He'd been a surgeon before Parkinson's took that away too. Now he wore a gaily patterned Hawaiian shirt. And the world's largest, goofiest grin.

"Dad?" I said. So I hadn't been hallucinating on the highway, though I still couldn't believe my eyes. He was an old guy, yes, with liver spots, but not as old as he'd been when I'd last seen him. It was as if he'd been frozen somewhere around retirement. There was still hair on his balding head, and some of it was brown.

"Honey," he said, a little sheepishly. "You found me."

I turned to Walker. Was this an acid flashback? Had I gone out of my mind? But he just shrugged. He'd seen it all, Walker's shrug said. We've lived together a long time.

"Hello, Howie," Walker said to my father.

"Walker, son. The two of you must join us," said my father. "It's a lovely feast."

That "you" and "us" nearly killed me.

"It's treyf, Daddy," I said. I said it lightly, without, I hoped, the meanness I felt in my heart.

"Shhh, honey," my father said, with a wink and smile, looking up at the sky. "He'll hear you."

His date laughed. She threw back her head, displaying her pretty throat. Clearly, she would laugh at anything, just to show it off. A swan's neck.

"This is Evangeline," said my father, introducing us. "We're in love," he said, as if that much weren't self-evident. "Being with her here," his hand fanned out to encompass the sea, the sky, the wine, the food, "it's not hard. Before it was hard, even with you, sweetie," he said to me. "My second favorite."

"You must be Anna," Evangeline said.

My father liked my older brother best. The drug addict, my younger brother, not so much.

"She was a sweet girl," said my father, as if I weren't there. "But that crazy career. The fagelah she married. This one," he pointed to Walker. "Smart, but he could never make a penny. I had to pay for their daughter's school."

That last swipe at Walker burned me up.

"What on earth are you doing here?" I said. "Slurping oysters? All these years I've longed for you."

My father smiled. "Always a flair for the dramatic. That's your gift. And you," he said, pushing it further with Walker, "how's the directing business?"

In his seat, Walker straightened his back, rising to his full height, which is tall, even in a chair. "Just fine. It's going swimmingly." He looked my father in the eyes. "That's a nice bottle of wine there, Howie," said Walker. It was a Muscadet sur Lie.

"What's mine is yours, Walker," said my father. "You know that."

Walker picked up the bottle and gave us both a healthy pour. He took a deep, indulgent sip. "I guess that's true," said Walker, slowly, the wine revving him up. "Your wife was yours, then ours."

After my father died, we'd taken care of her for years. For a while, when Kate was off at school, Mom had even lived in the little maid's room that had served as Kate's tiny bedroom, until, even with help, we couldn't handle her at home. Things had gotten so bad she no longer knew who I was. The bedpans and the bedsores. The diapers. Sometimes, while I was feeding her, no matter how many times we suffered through the ordeal of taking her to the dentist, a rotted tooth would fall out of her mouth.

Walker reached his hand out across the table and rested it on my right forearm, which like the rest of me was shaking. "That malpractice suit, the screw-up with your taxes, your drug addict son, and the other one, the greedy one. We seemed to inherit him too."

He gestured toward my chest.

"We could have used your surgical know-how a few years back, me and Annie."

My father sadly shook his head.

"Walker, Walker, you know most lives end mid-sentence," Dad said. "It was that way with my parents too. Muddles to clean up, scores and estates to settle. There's always more work to do."

"You don't look as if you're working, Howie," said Walker.

My father shook his head. He smiled ruefully, as if Walker was a child, which even now, in comparison to my father, he was. No matter how old we got, we would always be his children.

My father picked up the bottle. He poured us each another glass. We'd both inhaled the last round.

He turned to me, "What happened to your mother?"

"What do you think, Daddy?" I said. "She was beside herself without you."

"She played around with the will," he said. "That much I heard."

"It was a nightmare for Anna," said Walker, his face turning an alcoholic red. But I shushed him. This was my father, my battle. Already, I felt guilty for how much of Walker's time had been sucked up by my family's lunacy.

"The boys are suing each other over your money," I said. "It's one of the reasons we fled to France. No forwarding address."

"Me too," said Dad. He and his Evangeline shared a private look, and then they laughed and laughed.

"None of us even speak," I said.

He shook his head, sadly.

"How could you leave me with that?"

My father reached across the table, took Evangeline's hand in his.

"I'm in a better place," Dad said.

After lunch, we bade our farewells. My father kissed me on my forehead, and he held my wrist too, for a moment, until I realized he was taking my pulse, like he sometimes used to do when we all lived together back in Stuyvesant Town, and I shook it free. I was angry, sure, but that wasn't the half of it.

"I miss you, Daddy," I said, and meant it. I missed him more than I knew. I missed him so much I could feel the liquid in the center of my bones. More, I missed who I used to be back when I was still his daughter, a person with someone between her and God, a layer of protection floating like a cloud above me.

"It is what it is," said my father. "What can you do? Try to think about what's good." Then he and Evangeline walked hand in hand down the boardwalk away from me and Walker.

After that, there wasn't much else to do. I'd had enough of mourning and remembrance for one day, so we decided to skip the military graveyards. We got back into our rental car; we'd only leased it for the weekend.

"Can you believe it?" I said to Walker, seatbelt on, when we hit the road.

"I'm at a point in my life where I'll believe almost anything," said Walker. And then, more thoughtfully, "I suppose after all the time we've clocked, it makes sense that eventually I'd slip inside one of your delusions."

"Did he always talk in clichés, that way?" I asked.

"You tell me," said Walker.

We drove pretty much in silence back to Paris. What more was there to say? Walker had stood up for me. I took his hand and gave it a little squeeze.

Hours later, finally back in our apartment, I kicked off my shoes and broke out the wine, a nice red Sancerre we'd been saving, some Italian crackers and good French cheese, pears that I'd bought green, which were perfectly on point upon our return, so I sliced them. Dates and pistachios. A box of chocolates, a gift from one of Walker's dancers. I set it all out on mismatched china on our coffee table, put on a jazz CD Walker was fond of, and lit some candles. No need to turn on the lights.

Walker came out of the bedroom in his boxers, slipping a clean t-shirt over his handsome head. He'd washed his face and looked fresher, more boyish. I handed him a glass of wine and he smiled. I felt that smile travel all the way through my eyes and down my spine and shiver into my knees. This much I wished for Kate and Lucinda. Marriage is a miracle when it works.

That's when we decided to go home, once Walker's show was safely mounted, the following month. He'd received an email over the weekend offering him a spot in the Williamstown festival, so he'd be going back to something good, and there was hope for bringing the Paris Opera thing to BAM. The few days away had proved curative, and provided me an idea for a crucial scene I lacked. I felt for the first time in forever that I could be truly productive back in New York. I texted as much to dear Kate as we sat on the couch together, Walker and I, as we had for so many evenings over so many years, drinking wine, listening to the music, Walker's arm heavy and warm around my shoulder, his scent, musky and male, with a hint of soap, his very being silently sustaining me as I composed. We missed her so, I wrote, using both my thumbs, and time was marching goddamned fast. We loved her even more.

Cento for the Night I Said, "I Love You"

Like black birds pushing against glass,

I didn't hold myself back. I gave in completely and went

all the way to the vague influence of the distant stars.

I saw something like an angel

spread across the horizon like some dreadful prophecy

refusing to be contained, to accept limits.

She said, "Are you sure you know what you're doing?"

[This poem comprises lines borrowed from the following poets: Lucille Clifton, C. P. Cavafy, Rainer Maria Rilke, Raúl Zurita, August Kleinzahler, Louise Glück and Victoria Redel, respectively.]

RICHARD SIME

First Encounter

Make a drawing of it, I was told
My world of simple sun, bare land
She was raised in that kennel on the hill
An old trailer, I draw it vertical, tipped up on its rear end
There's plenty light but little shade
I add some frenchified shadow around the trailer
A loud squeak, ka-pow! its door is opened
I watch, standing in the foreground
Me, the benefactor, but I can't draw him either
A lone figure descends the trailer's steps
Dark, shapeless mass on its hip
What has he gotten into?
Blindness bird-dogs everyone
The eyeless mass takes shape: head   tail   paws
Her yet-to-be-discovered decency
She's thrust into his arms
He feels passion, pushed aside
One day he'll weep into her belly
Perspective is a gift I have not mastered

BRUCE SMITH

Raccoon

A man with CRCK on his snapback. A man in a BLDBTH hoodie
[what happened to the affable vowels?]. I stay shy of the men on the bus
because we know who we are. We are propelled by kimchi and cologne
that smells of diesel fuel and demon. Five hours of trance and hard
consonants. I find a seat next to Grace Paley, lit by a tiny beam,
who asks, Is there room for the unredeemed? She offers me a hard candy,
says, Do the dead ride for free? She points to the moon, Can we
have one of them, please, for everyone with a cookie? And then we
do what the dead, discounted do, we open a thin, neat bound book
and read as if that would feed or suffer or cut someone with
its white pages. Heat and the damp flames of us subtract the oxygen
from the air that boredom sharpened into despair. This is the time
between the shy, nocturnal creatures with dilated eyes and the diminished
ones that ransack the burnt over places. We stop at Big Daddy's to pick up
the escapees from the second and third great awakenings. These visionaries
have seen the ruby of the brake lights and have gone forward to be shattered
and to be known by Grace. They have bundled and touched one another
in a marriage sanctioned by the vowels of the Onondaga Nation.
Could each of us have, please, a more modest incline and a moon
we could douse like a raccoon douses its food? Its name means
puts its hands on everything. On this bus a creature was invented and
   carried
and crucified, a flesh cargo who dies in the five hour ride and vanishes
in the lights of the oncoming and in the fundamentalist war between
breath and distance. It [bus, breath, voice, distance] is a longhouse
that smells like a city of roasting meats, smothered fires, sewage
and perfumes, where hate and pleasure can live, almost cordially
if we relinquish our convictions. The invention of need in a lost language
happened here with a word or two doused in the dark. A woman
with a piece of toast who shivers. A woman with opera mask slippers.
And then a word that fails as soon as it is spoken, an exhaustion
that's a form of pleasure, although Grace says, *whose pleasure? whose*
   work?

JASON SOMMER
Grudge

The last of a late night's argument,
the dreadful unsnarling of intent—
our *what you said* and *what I meant,*
and neither of us penitent.
After the hours and anger spent,
what I continue to resent
there in the bed, the dark apartment
taking its turn as the respondent—
babbling pipes, sighing vent—
is how, some sliver of a moment,
sleep comes for you, and for me doesn't.

ARTHUR SZE
Black Center

Green tips of tulips are rising out of the earth—
you don't flense a whale or fire at beer cans

in an arroyo but catch the budding
tips of pear branches and wonder what

it's like to live along a purling edge of spring.
Jefferson once tried to assemble a mastodon

skeleton on the White House floor but,
with pieces missing, failed to sequence the bones;

when the last speaker of a language dies,
a hue vanishes from the spectrum of visible light.

Last night, you sped past revolving and flashing
red, blue, and white lights along the road—

a wildfire in the dark; though no one
you knew was taken in the midnight ambulance,

an arrow struck a bull's eye and quivered
in its shaft: one minute gratitude rises

like water from an underground lake;
another, dissolution gnaws from a black center.

ROSANNA WARREN
Augusting

Old news: leaf parchment crackles underfoot.
Pine needles, acorns, lichen. The waterfall
only a patter sliming the cliff.
The slope rumples down through mountain laurel
and pitches below to ramparts of slate,
shattered quarries, a moss-streaked bluff.
We tread on silver flakes and shadows.
Downward, ever downward, to the meadow
where the ghost lily, late summer wraith,
gapes, ash-pink, with news
of the underworld dusted on its tongue.

Another Life (Hawthornden, Midlothian)

from Thresholds

Eating a sandwich at the desk at the window
tracing the oak's bare winter branching
the thick lacing network is more an illusion
unhindered by the system's like extensions
no constraint to the path each finds in the air.

Gray fissured bark makes home for the lichen
mosses liverwort & the merveille du jour
that stimulates overgrowth into blistering gall
for nut weevil carabid pearly fritillary
chaffinch creeper warbler wasp.

I can see the bud clusters their scales on the twig tips.
The deep cold transfers through the old pane
its little waves rolling as I move my head
turning away to wrap up in scarf
a goshawk drops down to watch me eat
the branch he takes stand in comes so near
the hooked bill & talons make a new sentence.
His blue-gray blazon seems warm & proud
the white eye stripe a mask of power
on a holy man ready to seize the kingdom.
Las, qu'i non sun sparvir, astur!
Oh, to be a sparrow hawk, a goshawk
winging across to the lady I love!
If the casement were open I could almost reach him.
Could I be more than I am to my loved ones?
Could I be other than I am to anyone?
The minutes scatter to avoid his stare.
Small nosy things make their nest inside me
and the window kept closed keeps the hawk there.

C. K. WILLIAMS
Friends

Those of you who've gone before how precious
you remain how little your essential nature
has altered and insofar as it has I can't grasp

how you might be other than you ever were
surely you aren't wholly "gone" though that's
undeniably your essence now to have gone

surely you haven't even metaphorically risen
or descended it's just that you're not *available*
to those left behind unavailable for what

except the generation of future memories
I don't know that's the painful aspect of love
gone to no longer generate memories to share

here we laughed here danced all falls away
only the tattered snatches of what we call past
echo out from the isolate provinces of time

DAVID WOJAHN
Two-Minute Film of the Last Tasmanian Tiger

after Rilke

His vision, from the constant cascade of chicken wire, has grown
    So benumbed it contains
Nothing else, save for his *lastness*, though he doesn't know this.
    Yet he knows, in the manner
That beasts can know, that his name is *Benjamin*, & the name
    Comes with meat scraps, slotted

Through the wire by an aproned figure who is headless in
    The grainy black & white.
A zoo in Hobart, 1933. On his haunches he rises,
    Kangaroo-like, following
The movement of the keeper's hand. Look closely & you see the scar
    Where the mouth of a trap

Slammed its teeth into his left rear leg. Nothing tiger-like,
    Save the vague black ribbing
Of stripe along his rump. The size & shape of your average
    Retriever or Lab, though more forlorn.
& he paces his cramped circles, though no mighty will stands
    Paralyzed. Official moniker:

Thylacine. As he rises again to his haunches we glimpse
    The marsupial scrotal sack,
The pouch to protect his jewels as he padded the outback
    Bush he'll never see again.
& now the ears perk up, the curtain of the pupils parts & the mouth,
    The storied mouth,

The jaws hinging open, wider than those of any other mammal,
    Quickens in *the threat-yawn response,*
The cavernous throat. Benjamin, *Benjamin,* proffering abyss.
    Tiger, tiger burning the bright

Blacklit void. Our tour guide, our madly pacing limping Vergil.
     For three years more he paces

 & rears, paces & rears, chicken parts swallowed from the disembodied
     Chainmailed hand. His kidneys
Will fail, sarcoptic mange will mottle his stripes & torso to a scabbed
     Relief map, directions to Terra Incognita.
& thus his skin was deemed to be "of such poor condition"
     No attempt was made to stuff him.

DEAN YOUNG
Solar Plexus

I wonder what Tomaz is doing
in the afterlife. It's not totally
dark yet here but my shadow
is getting pretty confident.
There wasn't a window here before
but there is now. I know I'm nothing
but a drop of water but not if
I'm rain or dew or a tear from a stone eye.
The scariest part of the movie
is when a nearly featureless face
appears behind the star's face in the mirror.
Then all those wind-ups
start marching and tumbling and drumming.
Smoke comes out of a head
but that's nothing. A spiral
turns out to be a black horse
and sorrow proves too big for one body,
too big for all our bodies. Tomaz's
last postcard said either the lake
is volcanic or the cake is. If anyone
deserves to look Quetzalcoatl in the eye,
it's Tomaz. Hell, he had dinner with Mary
every Tuesday that semester I was mostly
in the hospital and the night I got
a new heart, he led our students in a chant.
Of course it hurt. Still does. And will
as long as I stay lucky.

LYNN SLOAN
Grow Animals

On the plastic monthly calendar stuck to the refrigerator, Michelle hadn't bothered to write the dates in the little boxes. Monday was Monday, Tuesday was Tuesday. The dates didn't matter. Desmond's routine filled the days: school=red dots, occupational therapy=orange dots, water therapy=green dots, speech therapy=yellow and brown checked dots. The stickers formed a lively zigzag pattern when Michelle squinted, even though it was all routine. Her own few appointments were made when Desmond was in school, so these she didn't mark down. The point of the calendar was to teach her son about time. Desmond, at six, was not, and would never be, OK in the way that OK was generally thought of. The blue dots at the bottom of the Friday lineup she added three weeks ago, after her eHarmony meltdown, when Henry, her brother, started coming over for dinner, "if you don't mind feeding me," pretending his visits weren't missions of mercy. She didn't know what was worse, that her younger, dweeb brother felt sorry for her or that she felt grateful.

She took out plates for dinner. "Make way, buddy," she said to Desmond, behind her.

Working the joystick, he backed up his wheelchair so she could walk between the cupboard and dining room.

With the dining-room table set, she sat on the kitchen stool opposite Desmond, uncurled his tight grip on the control wand of his chair and massaged his hand until it opened. She aligned her palm with his, lined up her long fingers with his small rigid ones, and slowly threaded hers through his until he grinned. Then she pulled away, her fingertips lingering on his until she lifted her hand and waved—their old game, played since before words made any sense to him. She began again, her palm to his, her fingers with his, twisted together, pulled apart.

He looked up at her, his jaw trembling. He was learning to talk and every word was an agony of effort.

"Mar...ee...Hen?"

Marry? She lowered her forehead to his, rolling her head from side to side, murmuring no. *Et tu, Desmond?* Henry had brainwashed her son when he babysat during her miserable eHarmony dates. Ever since, Desmond would ask about her getting married whenever Henry was due, or when any man crossed their path—the aging hippie with the grimy ponytail who lived across the hall, the grocery delivery guy, the gay receptionist at the rehab clinic they visited three times a week. Possibly Desmond's question was a cover for his real question: why didn't he have a dad? Sperm donor was not a concept he could understand, maybe never.

"You can't marry your brother, silly. And besides, you are my one and only."

"Love…Hen…?"

"I do love Uncle Henry." She stood up to peer in the oven at the lasagna, evading Desmond's watery brown eyes. "And Poppa and Nona," whom she avoided as much as possible because of how jittery they became around Desmond. "And Maybelline," their snarling, blind Airedale bitch.

The doorbell rang, two longs and one short. Henry. Desmond squealed, spun his wheelchair around, and zoomed down the hallway toward the front door.

"Slow down." He couldn't turn the knobs.

She poured her first glass of wine, enjoying the lovely gurgling sound. She'd been waiting for this moment, but she refused to drink alone. Before Desmond, BD, rules about small stuff were the mark of boring people. AD: Establishing and maintaining rules were essential. And besides, Desmond slept with a monitor. She couldn't take a chance.

The wine, tart and chill on the tip of her tongue, curling along the back, sliding down her throat, eased the tightness she never noticed until it loosened. She loved this moment that seemed to promise goodness ahead. True, on any given Friday night BD, she wouldn't be eating fattening lasagna and sipping no-buzz white wine. She'd be slamming through her closet to find the right skimpy dress and killer heels.

Self-pity is pathetic, Michelle.

Desmond wheeled back so she could unbolt the door. "Hen…"

Henry blinked, as if he'd forgotten who she was or why he had come, then his pudding face widened in a grin. He knuckled her head, his greeting ever since he reached six feet four in middle school and she, a senior in high school, remained locked at four eleven. From then on, he seemed to think he was her big brother, beginning with stink-bombing Nic Sage's convertible after Nic stood up Michelle, July 4th, the summer before she left for college. When Desmond was born, Henry had moved downtown into her neighborhood "in case of emergency."

"Yo, Mich." His sleepy eyes and too-big chin made him look stupid, but he was a crack programmer for a gaming company. Spying Desmond behind her, he intoned, "It's Henrik, Prince Henrik zee Evil Von," and swatted her thigh with the Kurt's Krafts bag he carried, to make her get out of the way.

Desmond collapsed in paroxysms of delight. Henrik, a mash-up of Dr. Spock and a movie Nazi, was Desmond's favorite of Henry's many roles, which included a blind, lisping physical therapist, who would mistake Desmond's ear for his nose; a pirate; and some monsters who made weird sounds inspired by Henry's games. Desmond butted his wheelchair into the back of her legs and grabbed for the Kurt's bag, knowing it was for him.

Henry yanked it out of range. "Zees are for later, for za shower. Ve have un whole zoo." He handed Michelle the sack, grabbed the handles of Desmond's wheelchair, and careened down the hall toward the living room.

Inside the Kurt's bag, she found a bunch of those capsules that dissolve in water and release spongy creatures. Grow animals. Desmond adored them. She tossed the bag in the bathroom—just once, she'd like a surprise for herself—and headed to the kitchen. A surprise for her? What a jerk. She paused at the hall mirror.

Lose the frowny face, Michelle.

In her early thirties, when her friends began to peel off into MarriedLand, and the unattached male herd began to thin, she had taken a serious look at her future and decided that what she wanted was a child, not marriage, not enduring coupledom. Her friends found her decision to be "totally cool," "courageous," "blasted awesome." But AD, these same friends dropped away, their lives so different. How could they enjoy sharing their worries and aspirations for their children when confronted with Desmond? She was lucky to have a brother like Henry.

Lose the clown grin, Michelle.

She had a son she loved. She worked from home in a condo she could afford, had a decent job maintaining sales and inventory for TRAK TEK, a company that sold used auto parts overseas. It wasn't branding and marketing, make-a-bundle-spend-a-bundle, expensive parties and river cruises, her job BD, but she could care for her boy. And every two weeks, when she went into the office, handsome Rivas in Systems, who never wore socks, not even in winter, and whose ankles were as beautiful as anything by Brancusi, he, Rivas, would say hello. Rivas, the married office flirt.

Michelle, you are pathetic.

Lasagna on the table, beer poured for Henry, milk in Desmond's sippy cup, her wine topped up, Michelle called them to the table.

Henry gorilla-grunted as he wheeled a sputtering and giggling Desmond to the table.

Her heart cracked open. Wishing her son's whole life could be all giggles, she strapped on his spork, tied on his "Da Boss" apron, and dished up the lasagna.

Henry loped around the table pawing his armpits.

"Settle down, Henry. You're egging Desmond on."

Both of them laughed at her, Desmond knocking his sippy cup sideways and Henry righting it. She asked if either of them would like salad, knowing they wouldn't, and the leftovers would be her lunch tomorrow.

"Salad, pallid, po bad it," Henry sang. "Nee naw no na nee."

Desmond sputtered out his first bite of lasagna. With her napkin she wiped his face and glared at Henry, who pretended to be chastened, then launched into a description of a new game someone, not he, was developing—time travel, massive weaponry, the usual.

Dinner was never pretty, but with Henry mimicking Desmond's jerky movements, tomato sauce and ricotta flew everywhere. At least Henry would shower Desmond afterward, a huge kindness. When Desmond graduated to a wheelchair, she'd taken out the tub, installed a walk-in, roll-in shower with a hand-spray, and bought a shower seat. Even so, bath times were increasingly difficult. He would twist and flay against the water's spray, sometimes bruising her. And he got erections. All boys do, the therapist said, even six-year-olds. What would she do when the hormones really kicked in?

She sipped her wine, half listening as Henry droned on about medieval armor.

Desmond interrupted. "I want…knight…with…hose."

"Steed, Sir Desmond, a manly steed ye be wanting. Axel be his name."

"Axel, I like that name," Michelle said, picturing her son in full knight's regalia, upright and gallant in the saddle, his wheelchair having morphed into a black stallion, shaffron and crinet gleaming.

Desmond touched his chest with his curled hand. "Sir... Desmond." He pointed to her. "Mmm?"

"She be Maid Michelle."

"Not me." She downed the last of her wine. "Maid" was too accurate. She went to the kitchen to retrieve the wine bottle. Two glasses—three actually—wouldn't be too much. She handed Henry a fresh beer.

He tipped back in his chair, took a long swig, and said, "Big news. A gamer's convention in Hong Kong, and I'll be there. Totally comped. With the fifteen-hour flight, makes sense to hang with some buddies in Jakarta after, and maybe swing by Bali."

Air squeezed from her lungs. He was abandoning her. "You in swim trunks?" she said.

He flat-eyed her as Desmond said, "I...swim."

"You're a dolphin, my man." Back to her. "I'll be gone six weeks, maybe longer."

Six weeks? She struggled to keep her face blank. Without Henry, she was alone.

Clingy is the public face of pathetic.

"Send us some pictures," she said, kicking back a slug of wine.

Henry said, "Des, my man, cover your ears. I want to talk privately"—he wiggled his eyebrows—"with your mom."

Desmond closed his eyes and began to hum as he patted the table with his spork-strapped hand, agreeably deserting her too.

"I signed you up," Henry said, she could barely hear him over Desmond's racket, "with another dating site."

"Oh, shit, Henry." Her betraying baby brother. "Which email d'you use? I'll close it down."

"Fair Maid Michelle, you be live at this very moment."

"Asshole."

"Listen, Michelle," he leaned forward, his face looking sincerely stupid. "It's a site for single parents with special needs kids."

"A tragedy troll site? You really are the Evil One. Do they put little angels next to everyone's lying photos and extra angel wings for each disability your kid has? Dammit, Henry. I'm fine."

"You are forty-one, way too young to let your twat shrivel."

"You are disgusting. You are not allowed to know that I have a twat."
Desmond's eyes sprang open.

"Bath time," she almost shouted, reaching across the table to wipe tomato sauce from his chin. Too hard. He winced and she hated herself. "Sorry, buddy."

Henry said, "You'll be hearing from some men, which is better, admit it, better than the sound of..." he wiggled his eyebrows again, "the sound of silent tears."

"Eighth grade, right?" she said. "Wasn't that your theme song in eighth grade?"

Ignoring her, Henry unstrapped Desmond's spork, tugged off his apron, flipped off the brake lock, then turned the wheelchair toward the hall. "Sir Desmond, Maid Michelle needs a time out. You and I will see if we can grow you a manly steed."

"Asshole."

From the kitchen she listened to the squeals and splashes from the bathroom, her stomach curdling with self-pity, resenting that Henry's grow animals were a big hit. She slammed the dishwasher shut, glad that its loud grinding interrupted the sounds of happiness down the hall, and glanced at the wheelchair scuffs on the cabinets, then at the calendar with its irritating zigzag pattern. She ripped off the blue dots for Henry's visits and dropped them in the garbage.

Whatever site he'd found had to be a scam. For someone who earned his living in CyberLand, her brother could be remarkably naïve. Unattached men simply did not exist in the quote unquote special parents club. She'd explained this to him, describing the dried-up husks she encountered in her rounds with Desmond. Everyone, each and every man and woman, was withered, she too, which was why she'd decided to sign up with eHarmony. When she asked him to babysit, she'd told him in cringingly embarrassing detail—she'd drunk too much—that she wanted a man to tell her she was pretty; she wanted a man to touch her; she wanted her body to be the source of pleasure, again, and not simply a functional beast of burden. But in eHarmonyLand she found out that nonwithered men do not want a woman who comes with a sidecar of responsibilities, responsibilities like a son who would always come first. When she came home from her last eHarmony fiasco, Henry's moon-face sagged when she told him how the guy said he had to step outside the restaurant to take a call, and never came back. A good brother, her closest friend, but that didn't give him the right to mess in her business. Even if his site were legit, it had to be overwhelmingly full of lonely-hearts women. Most of the women in the special parents club were single-divorced, not like her, single-by-choice. Many men couldn't take a kid who would never grow up. Even if a miracle unattached man with a disabled kid did exist, he would be a dried-up husk too: a punctilious planner, a worrier, never any craziness, and no goddamn fun. Just like her. She, who used to juggle men like oranges, would now be alone for the rest of her life.

Michelle, the road to stupid philosophizing is paved with drink, and you are drunk.

She opened her computer, ignored the flashing email icon—damn Henry—and entered TRAK TEK's portal. The dishwasher coughed and knocked. Down the hall the shower stopped. There were thumps and muffled laughter as Henry dried Desmond and carried him to his bedroom. Drawers slid open and closed, whispers, Henry's murmur reading a story. Blinking red lines announced that TRAK TEK's shipment from Singapore had been delayed in customs. She sent out a batch of notices to customers.

"Find anyone interesting?"

She jumped.

Henry stood in the doorway, his shirt spotted from Desmond's shower.

"I'm working." She returned her gaze to the spreadsheet on her computer screen, trusting her fury was visible.

"Mich, come on, you're my take-no-prisoners idol. I've built avatars based on you. Don't wimp out."

She snapped shut her computer. "It's not OK what you did. Admit it."

"Admit you're lonely."

"Admit you're a jerk."

He knuckled her head. "Good night, Mich."

She didn't walk him to the door.

After logging out, she swayed down the hall—she was a pathetic mess, a self-pitying child who got bombed on watery, piss-colored wine—double-locked the front door, and slid the chain in place. The rattle of metal on metal, like a prison lockdown. She pressed her face against the door and vowed she would never, ever drink again.

Down the hall the dishwasher shuddered to its stop. Quiet. All was quiet, so quiet she could hear her exhalation whisper on the door. She lifted her head. Through the open window in the living room came the tinkle of door chimes. Mr. G's, it had to be, across the street and four floors down. Then nothing. Silence. No ricocheted words, no car doors slamming, no screeching tires, bursts of laughter, no boom when a truck hit the metal plates that covered the sinkhole at the corner, not even the whine of the expressway two blocks over. She brushed her hair away from her ears, setting off waves of dizziness, but still hearing nothing. The rest of the world might have dropped away. She could be alone in the universe.

Desmond? She lurched toward his bedroom, needing to make sure he still existed. Into his dark room she tiptoed, watched by the red eye of his security camera. She paused, dizzied by the dancing spots of light that floated above him, from the revolving lamp on his nightstand, then walked closer. He was asleep, curled under his Batman quilt. Strands of damp hair clung to his forehead. Knotted fingers, wrists bent inward, arms that wouldn't straighten, legs like rubber bands, bent spine, and so small. Her beautiful birdboy. She slid his arm beneath his quilt, and he made a sweet sound.

With her hand on the wall to guide her, she padded down the hall. The bathroom was a mess, wheelchair parked by the toilet, wet towels and Henry's shoe prints all over the floor, and enormous animal sponges stuck to the shower tiles. No steed—*broken promise, Bro?*—but an orange camel the size of her laptop, a turtle as big as a basketball, a yellow pterodactyl with a wingspan the reach of her arms, far bigger than any grow animals she'd ever seen. Where had Henry gotten them? Not from Kurt's, that was for sure.

A black lump covered half the floor drain. She'd clean up in the morning. She flicked off the hall light, then back on, for Desmond.

In her dark bedroom, she flopped onto her bed, kicked off her slippers, tugged off her clothes, and rolled under the covers, her head swimming. A line of light from the hall sliced across her face, but she was too tired to get up and shut her door. She glanced at Desmond's monitor. His shadowy bed was just visible beneath the moving spots of light. The monitor buzzed.

Tomorrow you are going to have one monster headache.

Something wakes her.

Eyes closed, she listens to Desmond's monitor. Normal. She holds her breath, hearing nothing but the monitor's hum, remembering the eerie silence earlier, she and this apartment cut off from the world.

She blinks her eyes open. Something stands at her door, silhouetted in the hall's light, something blurry and dark, not exactly a shape, not as definite as a shape, not solid, but not transparent either. She must be dreaming. Or it is the wine? But she isn't afraid. Whatever it is hovers in her doorway, its head almost touching the door's lintel. It does have a head, but no face, not one that she can make out through her slit eyes, and a narrow body with arms that reach to where its knees would be if it had knees. The thing glides across the room toward her bed. She squeezes her eyes shut and listens to her heart knocking loud enough for whatever it is to hear. Still, strangely, she isn't afraid. The sheet above her flutters and lifts, admitting a chill puff of moist air that mists over her skin, prickling the tips of her breasts while, beneath her, the mattress shifts. Whatever it is has gotten into bed with her. It weighs less than a man would weigh. Pretending to sleep—maybe she is asleep—she smells something. Water? Has the dishwasher flooded? The bathroom? But there's no sloshing or dripping. And the scent that surrounds her isn't tinged with the ancient-iron-pipe tang of their water or Desmond's bubble-gum soap. It's pure and clean. Moisture suffuses the cells of her skin. Her whole body, muscles, bones, her too-tight skull, her spine that holds her upright through every day that she works so hard, all of her is softening. Deep within, she feels the old pulse of yearning. The creature nestles close and cradles her belly, its arm soft and damp and as spongy as a grow animal. She turns toward him, eyes closed, smiling. Clouds must smell like this, those boundless puffy clouds that drift without movement until they are gone.

ABOUT ALAN SHAPIRO
A Profile by Emilia Phillips

Often, when I'm writing, I open up my Internet browser onto poems I've found to be particularly instructive or compellingly enigmatic, poems that connect me with the reasons and, indeed, the questions about why I write and return to poetry as a reader, a parishioner, a believer. I've collected these poems via links I've emailed myself or titles I've remembered, and sometimes, when I'm writing, I only open them—I almost don't have to read them—as if their power's volatile, in the air. In the fan of tabs, I feel as if I'm communing with some kind of poly-faced god, and each poem represents its different incarnations. I know the poems so well, know their switchbacks and shortcuts and thoroughfares, their grid and range and population, and yet they still surprise me, connect me to the essential reckonings, the bewilderments of being alive.

Call me superstitious, but I hesitate to reveal which poems constellate my heavens as I navigate my own wine-dark sea, but Alan Shapiro's "Wherever My Dead Go When I'm Not Remembering Them" has been such a prominent blue-brightness on my horizon that I feel I wouldn't be honoring the poem—or Alan—by keeping quiet about it. I've taken this poem to students in class after class, read it again and again in silence or out loud, again and again listened to Slate's audio of Alan reading the poem, and several times challenged it to be as relevant and potent after months away from it. I have never grown tired of this poem, even though it's been with me for several years now, and I expect it to continue to direct me, carry me, question and devastate me.

When I met Alan at the 2013 Bread Loaf Writers' Conference, where he was faculty and I was a fellow, I wanted to tell him about my love for the poem, but I worried about saying something or, worse, requesting it before his reading, a sin akin to yelling "Touch of Grey!" at a Grateful Dead concert. I never know how someone feels about their own poems and, as a poet, I know how a poem can have its own life, how it can distance itself from its maker like an old flame and become intimate with a reader, as if to make the poet jealous. As if it's saying: I've moved on. Or maybe, it's the poet that has.

I suppose I was also worried about saying something to Alan because, in some way, by talking about the poem with him, the ownership of that poem would revert to him (now I was jealous). By not saying something to Alan about his poem, I could carry on with the poem, could continue to believe it was speaking to me and only me.

> ...*maybe it's like a subway passenger*
> *on a platform in a dim lit station late*
> *at night between trains, after the trains have stopped—*
> *ahead only the faintest rumbling of*
> *the last one disappearing, and behind*
> *the dark you're looking down for any hint*
> *of light—where is it? why won't it come?*

But then, Alan's so funny and generous and welcoming. At Bread Loaf meals, he sat down in a gray hoodie sweatshirt, folded his elbows on the table, and talked (basketball, music, poems, whatever). In getting to know Alan, in getting to learn the ways in which he thinks about poetry, the cadences of his speaking voice, I realized how much more that first poem I'd encountered began to resonate with me, how it began to seem driven less by an idea than an empathetic and playful heart. And then he read the poem. He walked up to the microphone and read the poem I'd been wanting to hear. I hadn't mentioned or expected it and I sat in the audience and cried. I didn't shake, I didn't make a sound: I just listened, tears streaming down my face, to a poem about an imagined place where one waits until one of his dead arrives on a train for the duration of a recollection and then leaves.

Born and raised in Massachusetts, Alan Shapiro has published numerous collections of poetry, including *Reel to Reel* (2014) and *Night of the Republic* (2012), which are two of my favorite collections in the last five years. His lines seem like a twisting of logic, an entrance into a complication, a nuance, a thought. Of his writing practice, he said it's "the usual—one word after another." He's also the author of two memoirs, a novel, and a collection of craft essays, and he's a distinguished professor at the University of North Carolina at Chapel Hill. When I asked him who his mentors were, he cited J. V. Cunningham, Ken Fields, Donald Davie, and every poet he admires, including "all of the poets in this issue of *Ploughshares*, never mind the illustrious dead." But Alan sieves his poetry through the strata of culture, the high and the low. In a 2002 interview with *The Atlantic*, he said, "I want to be able to devise a way of writing that can make a place for all of those influences. The high and the low. The elevated, the demotic. The literary, the street slang. The popular culture, the high culture. All of that has to have a place in what I write, if what I write is an attempt to bring the whole soul into activity, as Coleridge says it ought to be. It's got to be impure if it's going to be good." It's exactly this balance—or, rather, teetering tonal, cultural, and prosodic imbalances—that makes me trust his poems, his voice, the way he steps fluidly in and out of spaces, the "paradise of absence." In his poem "Joy," he describes "What hides when held," which for me is what a good poem does, indeed what Alan Shapiro's poems do; they allow you to hold them and then they slip from your grasp so you keep reaching for them again and again.

ABOUT TOM SLEIGH
A Profile by Emilia Phillips

The first time I met Tom Sleigh, he was stealing my suitcase.

I had just gotten off a charter bus in Mérida, Mexico, where I'd be spending a week at a conference, and in the rush and shove of passengers, I lost sight of my black roller among the pile into which the driver was slinging luggage. When I finally spied it, distinguished only by its wear and scuff, it was rolling away toward a taxi with a man I recognized from the back of poetry books. I had all of his collections (even a first edition of his first book), and even though he's one of my favorite writers, I was completely paralyzed for a moment, stunned in that I'm-in-the-presence-of-a-capital-p-*Poet* way. But there he went with that loping gait of his and my bag full of clothes and toiletries and books, and how embarrassing it would be, I thought, if he made it back to the hotel, unzipped the bag, and found my well-worn copy of *Space Walk*, dog-eared and marked up with eager checks and notes.

"Tom!" I called, running after him. He wheeled around, squinting and smiling into the crowd. Feeling the fool as I reached him, I said, "You *are* Tom, right?"

He assured me he thought he was. When I told him he had my bag, he looked confused and then, examining it, laughed. It was this moment that I realized that Tom is one of the most approachable people on the planet. Later on, as I spent time with him in person and through correspondence, I realized that he is also one of the most generous mentors to young poets and students of poetry around. I can't tell you how many times I've been to an event where Tom's name has come up in conversation and someone has said, "Tom's the best!" or "I just love Tom!"

What makes him so approachable and generous, I think, is his intensity of attention, a trait demonstrated in face-to-face conversations as much as his poems. When I interviewed him in 2014 for *32 Poems*, he said: "No matter where I am, Iraq, Libya, Somalia, New York, I try to take people one at a time." He looks everyone in the eye and also looks at what others refuse to look at: he witnesses instead of watches. He writes of civilians in war zones, a lion pacing his zoo enclosure, the pupil of a dog floating in a gravity-free kitchen, of junkies in Southern California, cats swarming over abandoned tanks in Beirut, American politicians as the village idiots—of so many other consequential subjects and scenes—with an unsentimental yet conscientious precision wrought only from his immersion in experience, in the gaze. His imagery is photographic, but his language is never captionlike. He exposes rather than exposits, and whether or not he's being funny (and he often is, sometimes scathingly so), his timing of details and sounds is like that of a comedian: the pattern most interesting—most significant—when it's broken.

Born in Mount Pleasant, Texas, Tom Sleigh has worked as a journalist in some of the world's most war-torn countries, including Syria, Somalia, Iraq, and Libya. He's also the author of eight books of poetry, including *Station Zed* (2015), *Army Cats* (2011), and *Space Walk* (2007); a book of essays, *Interview with a Ghost* (2006); and a translation of Euripedes' *Herakles* (2001). He's taught at many institutions, most recently Hunter College. In the poetry workshop I took with him in Mexico, he stressed the idea, after D. W. Winnicott, that all writers have a "fundamental orientation toward language," and this orientation should be recognized, embraced, and challenged in equal measure in one's writing.

In the middle of our interview a few years ago, he wrote to me to say that, although we had nearly finished our conversation, he felt as if he could do a better interview and asked if we could scrap the three thousand words we already had. I later published nearly six thousand words of an entirely new conversation, but among the scrapped material is the following passage I wish I'd cobbled into the published piece, one in which Sleigh discusses poems that set out with something to say versus poems that seek to find what they need to say:

> *What I am interested in is what the language is discovering moment to moment as the lines unfold: something that lies beyond my own politics and biases in writing about politically charged subject matter. For me, this means the discovery of my subject as I write, and not from some prefab stance, or hell of opinions that I simply populate with more opinions. I've said this before, but maybe it bears repeating: the language relieves you of having to stand guard over your own opinions*

and convictions, and gives you access to reaches of thought and feeling you might not otherwise imagine. Which is risky, unpredictable, and not always easy to reconcile with your day-to-day political, emotional, or intellectual entanglements...If the language isn't interesting, there's no reason to demean your subject matter."

To me, this passage speaks to his utmost respect for others, the subjects of our poems and our days. He demands that, if we are to write about ourselves and others, we must first find a way to render those experiences in ways that are real. That doesn't mean the journalistic facts; rather, it means that we must pay attention—to all that can be seen, all that can't be seen—and be generous: to one another, to ourselves, to our world.

In the few years that I've known Tom, he has challenged me to always be a better poet poem to poem, to be a better citizen, both literary and worldly. He gave me urgent edits to the poems of my first book when I'd asked only for a blurb, wrote essay-length responses to my interview questions, guided me to crucial poets when I needed an example, reminded me how to stay sane in po biz, and sent me "are you doing okay?" emails when I most needed them. There have been so many times when I've admired the engagement, the empathy, and the attention of some poets' work, but then I've found poets underwhelming in comparison. Tom, however, lives his poems, his language, and that's perhaps why his accidental theft of my suitcase seems so appropriate, so apt a metaphor for his poetic work: he takes the world with him so he can give it back to us.

THE PROMISED LAND AND ITS DISCONTENTS: THE FICTION OF JOSHUA COHEN
A Look2 Essay by Paul Scott Stanfield

Jewish American fiction, only a small presence in the American literary landscape before World War II, quickly became a colossus in the decades after. Besides the prize-winning big three of Bellow, Malamud, and Roth, talents as diverse as Cynthia Ozick, Leonard Michaels, and Gerald Shapiro contributed to a collective body of work that managed to be simultaneously earthy and otherworldly, comical and tragic, brazenly candid and hermetically coded.

That body of work is still growing. Jewish lore and experience inform much of the work of Michael Chabon, Rebecca Goldstein, and Steve Stern, and gifted fiction writers still on the green side of forty— Gary Shteyngart, Myla Goldberg, Nathan Englander, Dara Horn, David Bezmozgis—bring to emergent Jewish culture (the Soviet Jewish emigration, the continuing vitality of the Orthodox community, guitar-slinging Reform rabbis) the same capacity for outrageous humor, for prophetic utterance, and for being outside-yet-inside that made some of the novels of their predecessors American classics.

Joshua Cohen (born 1980) is somewhat younger than Shteyngart and company. His 2015 novel, *Book of Numbers*, was the first of his books to appear in hardcover and to be brought out by a large publisher (Penguin Random House), but despite his relative youth, his is a lengthening bibliography: three novels, a novella, two collections of short fiction, and some less easily classifiable items. Prior to *Book of Numbers*, publishers of his work have ranged from small (Dalkey Archive) to very small (Twisted Spoon Press, Fugue State Press) to vanishingly small (The Cupboard, "a quarterly pamphlet of creative prose published in Lincoln, Nebraska").

Reviewers of *Book of Numbers* typically pointed out its ambition and its timeliness. The ambition had been discernible in Cohen's work all along, in the stretching of novelistic form, in the gymnastics of his sentences, and in the demands he made of his readers. The timeliness, though, marks a departure. *Book of Numbers* reads as the confessions, notes, drafts, and *disjecta membra* of one Joshua Cohen, a novelist (but with a birth year and a bibliography quite different from the author's) who has landed the job of ghostwriter for a different Joshua Cohen, this one an Internet billionaire along Zuckerberg-Page-Brin lines. A thrillerlike plot gradually burbles up around a character resembling Julian Assange and revelations akin to those made by Edward Snowden—hence the timeliness. The heart of the novel, though, lies in the encounter between the novelist Joshua Cohen, devoted to ink and paper ("If you're reading this on a screen, fuck off," the book opens), and the tech-savvy, geek-speaking cyber pioneer with whom he shares a name.

In the Torah, the Book of Numbers tells of what became of the Israelites between Sinai and entering Canaan; its namesake novel gives us a Joshua Cohen who has entered the Promised Land and a Joshua Cohen who is dying in the wilderness. In hundreds of ways, Cohen's novel makes us ask, what Promised Land is this, what wilderness? (That its climactic scene is at the Frankfurt Book Fair is all too perfect.)

This allusion to Jewish history and the traces of *Yiddishkeit* that adhere to both Joshua Cohens carry forward in *Book of Numbers* what had been a defining characteristic in Cohen's earlier books: his incorporating an extraordinary amount of Jewish learning, history, and culture into his fiction, especially in his two full-length novels, *Cadenza for the Schneidermann Violin Concerto* (2007) and *Witz* (2010). And like *Book of Numbers*, those novels are for a patient, attentive reader.

Cohen's readers not only need the same working familiarity with Jewishness that a reader of *Ulysses* needs with Irishness, they also need the same patience in tracking syntax through a labyrinth of subordinate clauses that a reader of *Swann's Way* needs. They need to follow the smoky plumes of consciousness the way a reader of *To the Lighthouse* does, and to recall ephemeral detail from many pages back the way a reader of *Ada* does. Cohen reads like the last High Modernist, or the first New High Modernist. In the age of the tweet and the video clip, when the novel is warned to be reader-friendly or risk extinction, Cohen's embrace of difficulty is bound to seem quixotic. *Book of Numbers,* one could say, is about just how quixotic it is. But anyone who finds the difficulty of Joyce, Proust, Woolf, and Nabokov worth the effort, or who feels the importance of those writers goes beyond their being a recognizable face for a book bag, will find Cohen's difficulty worth investigating.

The back cover of Cohen's first book, *The Quorum* (2005), describes its contents pithily: "10 stories / 6 dreams / 1 rant." The last item may be an undercount, for all the stories approach the condition of rant. Their speakers address us in tones that veer from apology to accusation, they plead for the world's blessing between bursts of indignation. Sometimes they hope merely to be understood for once. A young man writes a wild, unfinished letter to Franz Rosenzweig, the long-dead German Jewish mystical theologian; a note at its end tells us the young man leapt to his death, the unfinished letter his baffled father's only clue to what was going on with his son. A man tries to explain to his psychiatrist why he has compulsively purchased beds from a particular bed salesman. Solomon's thousand wives analyze their collective relationship with their husband-king.

Sometimes the speaker is an intermediary, trying to explain to an audience presumed hostile the extravagant actions of a third party. An advocate pleads before "a heavenly jury" for the righteousness of Reb Schrieben, a Torah scribe who has taken the unspeakable liberty of adding to the Law (his Eleventh Commandment: "Thou shalt not stick thy nose in the, pardon, tush of God"). A book reviewer asserts that the untitled, authorless volume of six million blank pages he has just received is "the best record of, and commentary on, the Holocaust this reviewer has yet encountered. […] So, what does it mean? Nothing, possibly. And what does it teach? Nothing maybe…But it is not mawkish. It is not patronizing. It's not insulting."

In the sixty-page story that concludes *The Quorum*, its one indisputable rant, a violinist interrupts his performance of a concerto to launch into an impassioned account of the piece's composer, Schneidermann, a friend of the violinist and a Holocaust survivor, who has disappeared and may be dead. This story, greatly expanded, became Cohen's first novel, *Cadenza for the Schneidermann Violin Concerto*. As a debut novel, it would be hard to beat for sheer oddity. For one thing, it is entirely in the form of an improvised soliloquy delivered from the stage by an aging and dyspeptic emigré musician, running without a break for 380 pages. Even more intriguingly, it utterly departs from the expectation that young writers write about the young. Balzac's *Lost Illusions* set the template: a young writer, highly educated and adrift in the metropolis after a provincial upbringing, oscillates between ambition and anomie, collects a gaggle of highly similar friends, including a Judas or two, naively commits and then painfully emerges from a mare's nest of professional and romantic gaffes. It works for both men and women—for extra points, choose a foreign setting—and there is your debut novel. Cohen has instead taken on the voice of the A.K., the *alter kocker*, defined by Leo Rosten in *The Joys of Yiddish* as "a crotchety, fussy, ineffectual old man," in the same vein as but even ruder than the American expression "old fart."

Laster (the A.K. violinist) belongs to the line of narrators who record, and sometimes defend, the work of more brilliant friends: Watson and Holmes, Zeitblom and Leverkühn in Mann's *Doctor Faustus*, the narrator and Roithamer in Thomas Bernhard's *Correction*. Laster lacks Watson's equanimity, but the anguished exasperation of Bernhard's narrators he has in plenty. His anguish is mainly for his friend Schneidermann, last seen walking out on a matinee of *Schindler's List*, having shouted out in "jeremiad-voice, Prophet-mode": "*You want Holocaust? Holocaust I've got! I survived! Who needs a matinee movie? Who wants to meet a real survivor? Who wants to pay 10 bucks to see a real survivor?*" His exasperation is with the New World, its stupid pleasures, its childish culture, its ignorance. Hence the A.K. note: "I'm worthless and the whole world it's mislaid its mental apparatus, lost the instructions and the markings and no one knows what's good and what's not anymore." Men of the Old World, of European Jewry and the musical culture of central Europe, Schneidermann and Laster can exist only uneasily in the New.

But what nostalgia can there be, after the Holocaust, for that Old World, its smoke, ash, disgrace, and humiliation? Exiled from a homeland where he was persecuted as an alien, lifelong practitioner of an art threatened with obsolescence, his dearest friend gone and perhaps dead, Laster is driven to conclude

> *that just as there is no use for music, there is no use for the Jews, for the Jew, for Jewishness, that music and the Jews they are both totally worthless, almost perfectly worthless, equally, and that's why they've been almost totally, perfectly, eradicated...*

As Schneidermann had put it, "music it is the Jew of art [...] the Jew he is the music of humanity," both "serving no purpose at all" but both inexplicably "still there." Laster is still there onstage as dawn breaks, his audience now the police and the press, waiting to see what he will do.

Cohen, young as he is, inhabits his old-man persona as if born to it; much of his work, not just *Cadenza*, is steeped in the vanishing or vanished, the traditions of classical music performance, the Yiddish language, the multiple cultures of European Jewry. His attitude does not tend to be reverential, though, or even nostalgic. Two short books published in 2007, both collaborations with the artist Michael Hafftka, show his relationship to Judaism to be as intimately vexed as was Joyce's with Irish Catholicism. *Aleph-Bet: An Alphabet for the Perplexed* contains two memoirlike stories and an essay on the *sophiyot*, the five letters of the Hebrew alphabet that take a different form when they occur at the end of a word. After a drily parodic survey of the scholarship on how these exceptions came to be, Cohen brings out the theory that an accidental effect of scribal practice simply hardened, over time, into an obligation that no one dared omit. Thus all religions, he argues, become encrusted with absurdities:

> *I am fascinated [...] by the way in which lapse, or the lack of deliberation, creates future practice, constitutes life. Here, amid the final forms [i.e., the sophiyot], is, to me, the horror of Jewishness, the terror of Judaism, is the worst of all observant and organized religion (and so, too, why I myself cannot be "religious" or observant in any traditional sense)—in the most minor microcosm.*

Cohen's relation to Zionism is no less complicated; his short novel, *A Heaven of Others*, is a theological fable that may also be a commentary on contemporary Israel. A ten-year-old boy, Jonathan Schwartzstein, wanders in an otherworldly landscape that he gradually understands is the Muslim heaven. Some cosmic missed exit brought Jonathan here, we learn, after a suicide bomber crashed through the window of a shoe store where Jonathan and his father were shopping. Jonathan sets out to find Muhammad, hoping for answers, but finds instead a boy his own age—the bomber, it seems, who as a martyr of his faith has received exactly the promised award, but seems as nonplussed as Jonathan. Near the book's end, Jonathan—his surname translates as "black stone," recalling the Ka'aba—finally erupts in anger that the "faithful" will have it that orthodoxy persists in the afterlife:

> *Listen and I will say what I have said. In this heaven as in any heaven I am no longer a Jew. In this heaven as in any heaven I am no more a Jew than I'm not. Jewful and Jewless. Listen. Then hear. Understand. To be religious in heaven is to be truly fanatic.*

Jonathan goes on to denounce "the self-elected elect, the self-chosen chosen, the self-righteously rightful inhabitants of this heaven" who have turned it into a region of unlikeness, arid and terrible, that reproduces the exclusions, barriers, and policing that mar the earth.

Cohen's earlier books, excellent as they are, do not quite prepare one for *Witz*. By far the lengthiest and most complex of his books, it may be the one a newcomer to his work would be least inclined to pick up, but it is also the one that most abundantly shows his abilities.

Long though it is (817 pages), its main action is readily summarized. On December 17, 1999, a son, Benjamin, is born to Israel and Hanna Israelien of New Jersey, who already have twelve daughters. A week later, on Christmas Eve, all the Jews in the United States die, except those who are first-born sons. Infant Ben is temporarily under the care of his grandfather in Florida (also a first-born son), until all the surviving first-born sons are gathered into a special institution by government command. When Passover comes in the spring, all of the first-born-son Jews die as well—except Ben. In the wake of this second catastrophe, almost all of the United States converts to Judaism (or adopts it, there being no Jews left to conduct any formal conversions).

Ben, who is maturing at a preternatural pace, is now a precious commodity. He is provided with a model of his family home, complete with women performing the roles of his mother and sisters, and groomed as a kind of royalty-celebrity; he is even engaged to the president's daughter. The wedding is to be held on the 4th of July in Las Vegas—here, Los Siegeles—but Ben lights out for the territory. He roams the southwest, then makes his way eastward, finding his way to his family's abandoned house in New Jersey, then reuniting with his ersatz mother and sisters. He has a spectacular, even mystical episode of cunnilingus with his ersatz mother (in the course of which his tongue is ripped out), news of which leaks out via a hotel maid, leading to his disgrace and fall. Now an outlaw, he flees to Poland, which has become "Polandland," owned and administered by the US as a kind of Old World theme park with a sinister purpose: those who have refused to become Jews are brought here to be put to death.

Ben next mysteriously emerges in "Palestein," which in the alternate universe of this novel is an Arab monarchy. He has grown horns. He has a visionary experience that ends, it appears, in his death. In the final chapter of this main story line of the book, a museum holds a gala event to celebrate the acquisition of a sacred relic—Ben's tongue.

The novel has a coda of some thirty pages in which the last living Holocaust survivor muses in unpunctuated, Molly-Bloom fashion over his past and present. He is 108, and the novel ends with the punch lines—*only* the punch lines—of 108 Jewish jokes. (*Witz* is Yiddish for "joke.")

The Jewish resonances, as is evident even in the summary, are innumerable. The disaster in which all Jews but first-born sons die is an inversion of the tenth plague visited upon the Egyptians in Exodus, with Santa Claus recast as the Angel of Death. Las Vegas' new name honors the Jewish gangster, Bugsy Siegel, whose vision it was to make the city a gambling and entertainment capital. Ben's oral sex with his ersatz mother, during which he winds up in her uterus and then reemerges, occurs on Tisha B'av ("The Ninth of Av"), the day on which both the First and Second Temples were destroyed, ever since a day of mourning, and according to some traditions the day on which the Messiah will be born. Ben's loss of his tongue matches the curse the speaker of Psalm 137 pronounces on himself should he "forget thee, Jerusalem" and sing the Lord's song for the entertainment of strangers. "Polandland" is an inversion of the Holocaust, in which Gentiles die for being Gentiles. Not to mention red heifers, the Third Temple, the echoes of the liturgy for Yom Kippur, or the way Cohen's description of the facility for Jewish first-borns is shot through with memories of both Ellis Island and the Nazi concentration camps.

While, on the one hand, *Witz* presents this kind of manic Jewish fabulism, on the other hand, it has set piece after set piece of beautifully nuanced realism: Israel and Hanna's wedding, the Florida apartment complex of Benjamin's grandfather, the Vegas hotel in "Los Siegeles," the museum gala. Alongside his novel's extravagant invention, Cohen is also very good at the kind of thing novelists like Trollope and Updike are good at—noticing and recording the way we live now, helping us to see our own world.

Cohen's prose, though, is not of a well-mannered Updikean limpidity. The characteristic *Witz* sentence is encyclopedic, maximalist, a quick-change artist doing the police in different voices, a river in flood that wants to caress every inch of every chicken coop, every tractor tire, every stick of driftwood that it is bearing away in its wake. It may take up most of a page. It usually embraces several tonal registers during its course, from the demotic to the epic, sometimes sounding fueled and riffing like Lenny Bruce, sometimes biblically ornate like Cormac McCarthy—if, that is, McCarthy peppered his prose with Yiddish and Hebrew.

Here is the conclusion of a sentence describing the plague-emptied Lower Manhattan that Benjamin encounters as he crosses from New Jersey into New York City via the Holland Tunnel:

> *[...] this season, menschs let out their bellies; womenfolk smear their makeup onto the faces of streets, pink and streaks of red like rainbows trailed by snails, then pray for an innerly inclement weather, asking the cloudfall to cool their lusts, to purify their souls; their kinder pitch pennies worthless into the sewer green and gold, dogs once theirs now stray dash lame from snow to snow...skyscrapers once new, abandoned to scaffolds; earthworming giants idle, dumpster hulks sanctifying as symbols of an emptiness within; ambition unfinished, thrusts unfulfilled; lorded over by an inutile silence and the holy stillness of cranes.*

Along with a sprinkling of Yiddish—the novel invariably uses "mensch" for "man" or "person," "kinder" for "children"—we get an image of dropping dead as a fashion trend, an image of made-up women collapsing on the street heightened with a simile both beautiful and queasy-making ("like rainbows trailed by snails"), then an image of orphaned children, not long to live themselves, and abandoned dogs in a stunning string of monosyllabic words ("dogs once theirs now stray dash lame from snow to snow") that almost sounds like a William Carlos Williams poem. Then Cohen piles up inverted absolute phrases that read like Whitman-out-of-Ginsberg ("earthworming giants idle, dumpster hulks sanctifying") before flipping in a wholly surprising but perfect French adjective and a final image that looks like the last line of a haiku until you realize it completes the picture of arrested construction.

Witz is not only a stylistic tour de force, though. The outlandish events at the center of the plot—the catastrophic dropping dead (in two distinct waves) of every Jew except Benjamin, the abrupt conversion of the whole population of the United States—are both logical if extreme extrapolations of circumstances that have ever-present realities for Judaism for a very long time.

There have, notoriously, been those who wished extinction on the Jews. Besides Hitler and the Nazis, of course, we have the czars and their pogroms, Ferdinand and Isabella, Ahasuerus, Pharaoh. The dying off suggests, perhaps, the realization of a desire certain Gentiles have entertained for millennia, with Santa Claus as the Angel of Death: "Most are expecting a stockinglike sack [...]. Tonight it's a can he carries, a metal battered can as if of paint; it's a bucket, for the record— filled with the blood of the lamb, cut with that of goats when the Arctic slaughterhouse went short on a stray flock."

But we could also read Santa—the American idol before whom a few more Jewish parents cave every generation—as the Angel of Assimilation. Is the dying off of every American Jew (save one) in *Witz* a figure for American Jews who in effect stop being Jews? A year after the plague Christmas, the administrator Die (one third of a triumvirate with Das and Der), presiding over the now empty Ellis Island Great Hall dormitory, celebrates Christmas with a tree, which accidentally catches fire. Cohen turns the fire into a trope for assimilation:

> *Understand, this is assimilation: the transference of one element to another, one state as to its voided other, fire to smoke, tree to ashing away on the wind that seeds, and sorrows...O if only that smoke, that ash, it all, could be reassembled into the lost, but how, made manifest and whole through some, any, allied alchemical effort...to be made then remade in perpetual recreation, what would that cost, what would that be worth—what's a resurrected life, especially when you have to buy new possessions, when you have to chase after new desires by which to become possessed all over again?*

"Holocaust" refers literally to complete destruction by fire; this fire points simultaneously to the destruction of European Jewry by the Nazis and to the cultural amnesia of American Jews as two different kinds of irrecoverable loss.

The monologue of the last living Holocaust survivor that concludes the book likewise links assimilation to fire, suggesting a kind of attenuation of tradition to almost nothing—"assimilationist tendencies from ash into air into academics and stories inventions the deconstructivist dated that's what we do we redact each and every storied second season bedded down in the ground in the air in the pole of the Himmelhow sky there's nowhere else to die nohow to sleep and yet why [...]."

The dying off could be interpreted, then, as an extrapolation and acceleration of a reality already slowly unfolding. In 1990—Cohen would have been ten years old—a National Jewish Population Survey found that 52 percent of American Jews married outside the faith, setting the stage for a "crisis of continuity." A crisis of continuity may be what those 108 punch lines at the novel's end are about. *The Joys of Yiddish* or *The Big Book of Jewish Humor* will furnish the novel's reader with the setup of each punch line (and the reader should take the trouble, because they are hilarious). But just as each punch line depends on its setup, one realizes, each joke depends on the context of Jewishness. So will the jokes mean anything as Jewishness evaporates in the bright American sunshine? Will they just be meaningless sentences some A.K. mumbles to an audience of no one?

The mass adoption of Judaism by American Gentiles in the wake of the great dying off could also be an extrapolation of processes long in motion. Before World War II, there was a wide, savage streak of unapologetic anti-Semitism in American culture, high and low. After World War II, we saw the embracing of Anne Frank, the lionization of Bellow and Roth, the universal popularity (until...) of Woody Allen, the Americanization of the bagel, Jewish US Senators, *Fiddler on the Roof*, Steven Spielberg.... Is Cohen making the bitter joke that *all it takes for Gentiles to embrace all things Jewish is the disappearance of Jews?* Of course, this obverse of assimilation is even older than that. An enormous chunk of Western culture is founded on just such an appropriation of Judaism by Gentile Christians, who took Judaism's sacred texts, renamed them the Old Testament, and claimed their stories, personages, and truths as their own.

The chief irony of *Witz* is that the *Yiddishkeit* that disappears from the novel's imagined world is infused into every detail of the novel itself. Joyce's famous boast that were Dublin destroyed, it could be rebuilt by consulting *Ulysses* was not really true even in 1922; nor could Jewish culture be reconstituted solely from *Witz*. But just as a reader feels the sensory plenitude of Dublin in *Ulysses*, so a reader of *Witz* is immersed in Jewish American experience (with the Internet, perhaps, doing the work it took generations of Joyce scholars to do by explaining such terms as *dayenu, tikkun olam*, and *hatikvah*). Combine that with the novel's embrace of the American landscape—Miami, Las Vegas, Hollywood, the Southwest, and of course New Jersey and the Lower East Side—and *Witz* begins to feel like a one-off American classic. If it finds enough readers, it will be.

Paul Scott Stanfield, educated at Grinnell College and Northwestern University, teaches in the English Department of Nebraska Wesleyan University and is the author of Yeats and Politics in the 1930s *(Macmillan, 1988) and various articles. He lives in Lincoln, Nebraska, with his wife, Barbara Straus, and plays bass and writes songs for local garage rock ensemble Prairie Psycho.*

Alice Hoffman Prize for Fiction

Alice Hoffman Prize for Fiction *Ploughshares* is pleased to present Ramona Ausubel with the fifth annual Alice Hoffman Prize for Fiction for her short story "Fresh Water from the Sea," which appeared in the Summer 2015 issue, guest-edited by Lauren Groff. The $1,000 award, given by acclaimed writer and *Ploughshares* advisory editor Alice Hoffman, honors the best piece of fiction published in the journal during the previous year.

About Ramona Ausubel and "Fresh Water from the Sea"
Ramona Ausubel's new novel *Sons and Daughters of Ease and Plenty* will be out in June 2016 from Riverhead Books. She is also the author of *No One Is Here Except All of Us* (Riverhead Books, 2012) and *A Guide to Being Born* (Riverhead Books, 2013). Her work has appeared in *The New Yorker, One Story, Electric Literature,* and elsewhere. She is currently a faculty member of the Low-Residency MFA program at the Institute of American Indian Arts.

What inspired "Fresh Water from the Sea"?
The very first version of the story sprang into my head when I was talking to a friend about an argument she had had with her mother, who was very different from my friend. My own mom and I are similar, and it struck me as an amazing truth that a person might give birth to someone utterly unlike herself and that a child might grow up in a family that she does not relate to.

Then, a few years later, my family and I spent a year in my hometown, which I have always loved and missed (I moved away when I was seventeen). Coming back was surprisingly sad. I missed missing home. Being a person at some distance from her upbringing had become part of my identity, and I didn't know quite who to be once I came back.

Somewhere in my brain, these two stories made sense together, and I chose to set it in Beirut because there are many more Lebanese people living outside Beirut than in it and it seemed like the ultimate missed home. I spent exactly two days there several years ago and otherwise my information is imagined.

What did you discover or grapple with while writing it?
I grappled with the mechanics of the mother's disappearance. I wanted a physical thing to happen, for the emptiness of not being able to miss her home anymore to actually make her body thin out, like a cloud. It took a long time to find the exact right imagery for this, for it to feel actual. Meanwhile, I worked to make the relationship between mother and daughter as sharply specific as possible, for the city to be all hard lines and real materials, for the years spent away to be a rich soil for the mother's nostalgia.

How does this story fit with the rest of your work?
"Fresh Water from the Sea" comes out of a new collection of stories I am finishing entitled *Awayland*. All of the stories take place in different parts of the world and are about people far from home in many different ways. Some are fantastical, like this one. There is an online dating profile written by a Cyclops and a story that enters the consciousness of a group of mummified animals and a story about three shipwrecked Vikings who discover a dying mermaid, and others. Whether there's magic or not, I'm always interested in the ways in which love forces us to stretch, sometimes in strange and unimaginable ways.

*Book Recommendations from
Our Advisory Editors*

Peter Ho Davies recommends *Angels of Detroit* by Christopher Hebert: "A rust belt epic by a writer of distinctive vision. More than a dozen years in the making—I saw the earliest iterations in workshop and have never forgotten them—it's been worth the wait."

Jane Hirshfield recommends *Practicing the Truth*, by Ellery Akers: "*Practicing the Truth* is a book of gorgeous knowledge and unlikely couplings. A scientist's precision marries a painter's eye marries a Whitmanesque inhabitance of all being—insects, leaves, rocks, weathers, the narratives of many lives, her own not taking precedence over others'. These honed, faceted, closely observed poems are no ordinary lyrics—they spring open the hidden wildness of both language and compassion. Akers publishes rarely—her first poetry book, *Knocking on the Earth*, came out in 1988. This is her second, selected by Alicia Ostriker for Autumn House Press's Poetry Prize."

Tony Hoagland recommends *The Four Legged Girl* by Dianne Seuss: "Seuss makes images like carnivorous flowers; she has enormous duende and psychic complexity, and every one of her poems is a vivid event of fluent and fierce imagination. This is a signature book of a large talent arriving at her stage of full wild-blown poetic strength."

Thomas Lux recommends *Where You Want To Be*, New and Selected Poems, Black Lawrence Press, by Kevin Pilkington: "Pilkington's understated poems, often hilarious, always original and lucid, have mattered to me and moved me for many years."

Joyce Peseroff recommends *Magpiety* by Melissa Green: "Green brings immense pressure to bear on every line—what she calls 'torque,' and which describes the coil of a spirit that responds to the world with painful frankness and breathtaking lyricism. *Magpiety* includes selections from Green's prize-winning first book, *The Squanicook Eclogues,* followed by published and unpublished work written during decades when the poet suffered from debilitating depression. Green's mastery of image, sound, and tone signals a unique voice that's been too long away."

Gerald Stern recommends *It Shouldn't Have Been Beautiful* by Lia Purpura: "Purpura's poems are accessible, strong, and important. She is one of the best of her generation."

Richard Tillinghast recommends *H Is for Hawk*, by Helen MacDonald: "The British excel at nature writing, and this is a fine book. Here is the beginning of a paragraph, chosen almost at random: 'In the half-light through the drawn curtains she sits on her perch, relaxed, hooded, extraordinary. Formidable talons, wicked, curved black beak, sleek, café-au-lait front streaked thickly with cocoa-coloured teardrops, looking for all the world like some cappuccino samurai. "Hello hawk," I whisper, and at the sound, she draws her feathers tight in alarm. "Hush," I tell myself, and the hawk. Hush.'"

Rosanna Warren recommends *Forgotten Country*, a novel by Catherine Chung: "In a clear and subtle style, Chung tells the story of a Korean family's immigration to the United States, the buried and not-so-buried sorrows they left behind, and the cross currents of their life in the new country. Key moments in the narrative are concentrated into images. The book's beauty lies in its quiet understatement and suggestiveness, while the story itself is harrowing."

EDITORS' CORNER
*New Works by Our
Advisory Editors*

Martín Espada, *Vivas to Those Who Have Failed,* poems (W. W. Norton, January 2016)

Thomas Lux, *To the Left of Time,* poems (Houghton Mifflin Harcourt, April, 2016)

Gail Mazur, *Forbidden City,* poems. (University of Chicago Press, March 2016)

Gary Soto, *You Kiss by Th' Book,* poems (Chronicle Books, Spring 2016)

CONTRIBUTORS' NOTES
Spring 2016

Elizabeth Arnold, winner of an Amy Lowell scholarship, a Whiting Writer's award, and fellowships from the Radcliffe Institute for Advanced Study, the Rockefeller Foundation, the Fine Arts Work Center, Yaddo, and MacDowell, has published four books of poetry, *The Reef* (University of Chicago Press,1999), *Civilization* (Flood Editions, 2006), *Effacement* (Flood Editions, 2010), and *Life* (Flood Editions, 2014). She teaches on the MFA faculty at the University of Maryland and lives in Hyattsville, Maryland.

L. S. Asekoff has published four books of poetry: *Dreams of a Work* (Orchises Press, 1994), *North Star* (Orchises Press, 1997), *The Gate of Horn* (TriQuarterly/Northwestern University Press, 2010), and the verse-novella *Freedom Hill* (Northwestern TriQuarterly/University Press, 2011). In 2012, he was chosen as a Witter Bynner Fellow to the Library of Congress by Poet Laureate Phil Levine. He received a Guggenheim Fellowship in 2013. He has recently completed two manuscripts: *Eclipse*, a collection of poems; and *Black Ship*, a book of prose poems and short prose pieces.

Peter Balakian is the author of seven books of poems and four books of prose. His recent books are *Ozone Journal* (University of Chicago Press, 2015) and *Vise and Shadow: Essays on the Lyric Imagination, Poetry, Art, and Culture* (University of Chicago Press, 2015). His memoir, *Black Dog* *of Fate* (Basic Books, 1997) won the PEN/Albrand Award. He directs the Creative Writing Program at Colgate University.

Ari Banias lives in the Bay Area and is a Stegner fellow in poetry at Stanford. The author of a chapbook, *What's Personal Is Being Here With All of You* (Portable Press, 2012), his poems have appeared in *American Poetry Review*, *The Feminist Wire*, *Guernica*, and elsewhere. His first collection of poems, *ANYBODY*, is forthcoming (W. W. Norton, 2016).

Charles Bardes is a physician who practices and teaches medicine in New York. His work has appeared in *AGNI*, *Literary Imagination*, *Proto*, *The New England Journal of Medicine*, and elsewhere. *Pale Faces: The Masks of Anemia* (Bellevue Literary Press, 2006) is a book-length rumination on the cultural and mythological aspects of this common disease construct. In 2008, he was the Bernard deVoto Fellow in Nonfiction at Bread Loaf Writers' Conference.

Catherine Barnett is the author of *The Game of Boxes* (Graywolf Press, 2012) winner of the James Laughlin Award, and *Into Perfect Spheres Such Holes Are Pierced* (Alice James Books, 2004). Her honors include a Whiting Writer's Award and a Guggenheim Fellowship. She teaches in graduate and undergraduate programs at NYU and Hunter College and works as an independent editor. She has degrees from the MFA Program for Writers at Warren Wilson College and from Princeton Univer-

sity, where she has taught as a lecturer in the Lewis Center for the Arts.

Michael Burkard is the author of *lucky coat anywhere* (Nightboat Books, 2011); *Envelope of Night: Selected and Uncollected Poems, 1966–1990* (Nightboat Books, 2008); and *Unsleeping* (Sarabande Books, 2001), among others.

Gabrielle Calvocoressi is the author of *The Last Time I Saw Amelia Earhart* (Persea, 2005) and *Apocalyptic Swing* (Persea, 2009). She is Senior Poetry Editor at *Los Angeles Review of Books*. She teaches in the Warren Wilson Program for Writers and at University of North Carolina at Chapel Hill. Her third book of poems, *Rocket Fantastic* is forthcoming in 2017.

Peter Campion is the author of three collections of poems, *Other People* (University of Chicago Press, 2005), *The Lions* (University of Chicago Press, 2009), and *El Dorado* (University of Chicago Press, 2013). The recipient of the Guggenheim Fellowship, as well as the Rome Prize from the American Academy of Arts and Letters, he directs the MFA program at the University of Minnesota.

Michael Chitwood's poetry and fiction have appeared in *The Atlantic Monthly*, *Poetry*, *The New Republic*, *Threepenny Review*, *Virginia Quarterly Review*, *Field*, *The Georgia Review*, and numerous other journals. *Gospel Road Going* (Tryon Publishing Company, 2002), a collection of poems about his native Appalachia, was awarded the 2003 Roanoke-Chowan Award for Poetry. *Spill* (Tupelo Press, 2007) was named as a finalist for *Foreword Reviews'* poetry book of the year and won the 2008 Roanoke-Chowan Award. His most recent collection, *Poor-Mouth Jubilee* (Tupelo Press, 2010), was also named a *Foreword Reviews* finalist. His latest book is *Living Wages* (Tupelo Press, 2014).

Andrea Cohen's most recent books are *Furs Not Mine* (Four Way Books, 2015) and *Kentucky Derby* (Salmon Poetry, 2011). *Four Way* will publish her fifth poetry collection in 2017. Cohen directs the Blacksmith House Poetry Series in Cambridge, Mass., and the Writers House at Merrimack College.

Michael Collier's sixth book of poems is *An Individual History* (W. W. Norton, 2014). A recipient of an Award in Literature from the American Academy of Arts and Letters, he teaches in the creative writing program at the University of Maryland and is director of the Bread Loaf Writers' Conferences.

C. L. Dallat, poet, musician, and critic, (b. Ballycastle, Co. Antrim, Ireland) now lives in London, where he reviews literature and the arts for the *TLS* and *The Guardian,* among others, and has been a regular contributor to BBC Radio 4's weekly *Saturday Review* since 1998. His first poetry collection was *Morning Star* (Lagan Press, 1998), he won the Strokestown International Poetry Competition in 2006, and his latest collection is *The Year of Not*

Dancing (Blackstaff Press, 2009). cahaldallat.com

Katherine Damm was raised in Philadelphia and now lives in Brooklyn. She attended Harvard University, where she was awarded the Harvard Monthly Prize for literary promise. She is working on a novel.

Susan Davis has published one book of poems, *I Was Building Up to Something* (Moon Tide Press, 2011). A second, *Feet Like Water Lilies,* is forthcoming. Her work has appeared in numerous journals, most recently the *Cincinnati Review.* She teaches creative writing at University of California, Irvine, and to students in the township of Kayamandi, South Africa.

Matthew Dickman lives and works in Portland, Oregon. His first book, *All-American Poem* won The Honickman First Book Prize, The May Sarton award from the American Acadamy of Arts and Sciences, and the 2009 Kate Tufts award. His latest book is *24 Hours* (Onestar Press, 2014). His poems have appeared in *Tin House, Dossier Magazine,* and *The New Yorker,* among other places.

Michael Dickman was born and raised in Portland, Oregon. His newest book of poems is *Green Migraine* (Copper Canyon Press, 2016).

Stuart Dischell's most recent book, *Backwards Days,* was published by Penguin in 2007. His first two books, *Good Hope Road* (Penguin, 1993) and *Evenings & Avenues* (Penguin, 1996), are being reissued in the Carnegie Mellon Contemporary Classics series. *Terminus Magazine* is serializing his nonfiction work *Walking the Walls of Paris*. He teaches in the MFA Program at Greensboro.

Camille T. Dungy is the author of *Smith Blue* (Southern Illinois University Press, 2011), *Suck on the Marrow* (Red Hen Press, 2010), *and What to Eat, What to Drink, What to Leave for Poison* (Red Hen Press, 2006). She edited *Black Nature: Four Centuries of African American Nature Poetry*, co-edited the *From the Fishouse* poetry anthology, and served as assistant editor for *Gathering Ground: A Reader Celebrating Cave Canem's First Decade*. Her honors include an American Book Award, two Northern California Book Awards, a California Book Award silver medal, a Sustainable Arts Foundation grant, and a fellowship from the NEA. Dungy is currently a professor in the English Department at Colorado State University.

Stephen Dunn is the author of seventeen books of poetry, including the recent *Lines of Defense* (W. W. Norton, 2014) and a chapbook *Keeper of Limits* (Sarabande Books, 2015). His many awards include the Pulitzer Prize, an Academy Award in Literature from the American Academy of Arts & Letters, and the Paterson Award for Sustained Literary Achievement. He lives in Frostburg, Md.

Tarfia Faizullah is the author of *Seam* (Southern Illinois University Press, 2014) and *Register of Illuminated Villages* (Graywolf, 2017). Her poems appear widely in periodicals and anthologies, and have been trans-lated into Chinese, Spanish, and Bengali. Her work has received numerous awards, including a Pushcart Prize and a Fulbright fellowship. Tarfia codirects the Organic Weapon Arts Chapbook Press & Video Series and is the Nicholas Delbanco Visiting Professor of Poetry at University of Michigan's Helen Zell Writers' Program.

Jerzy Ficowski (1924-2006) was a prolific poet, songwriter, and scholar on the Polish Roma population, as well as the life and work of Bruno Schulz. Recent translations of Ficowski's poems have appeared in *American Poetry Review, Poetry, The Nation, New York Review of Books,* and elsewhere.

Anne-Marie Fyfe's fifth poetry collection is *House of Small Absences* (Seren Books, 2015). Born in Cushendall, County Antrim, Ireland, Anne-Marie lives in London where she works as an arts organizer. She has won the Academi Cardiff International Poetry Prize, has run Coffee-House Poetry's event series at London's leading live literature venue, the Troubadour, since 1997, is Poetry Coordinator for the annual John Hewitt International Summer School in Armagh City, and is a former chair of the UK's Poetry Society. annemariefyfe.com

Kirby Gann's most recent novel, *Ghosting* (Ig Publishing, 2012), was named a Best of Year by *Publishers Weekly* and flavorpill.com. A freelance editor and book designer, he has been named Series Editor of Bookmarked—brief books in which authors address, in any way they desire, a classic work that proved formative to their writing. Gann and his wife, Stephanie, live in Louisville, Ky., where he is on faculty at the low-residency MFA Program at Spalding University.

Ross Gay usually lives in Bloomington, Ind., where he teaches poetry, gardens, instructs kettlebell classes, and does other stuff. This year, though, he has had a fellowship at the Radcliffe Institute, so he's renting a room in Cambridge, foraging unpicked apples down the street, and eating them with peanut butter. His most recent book is *Catalog of Unabashed Gratitude* (University of Pittsburgh Press, 2015).

David Gewanter is author of three poetry books, *War Bird* (University of Chicago Press, 2009), *The Sleep of Reason* (University of Chicago Press, 2003), and *In the Belly* (University of Chicago Press 1997) and coeditor of *Robert Lowell: Collected Poems* (FSG & Faber, 2007). Recent work appears in *Tikkun, Western Humanities Review, Agni,* and *Times Higher Education* (UK). Awards include the John Zacharis, Witter Bynner, Whiting, and James Laughlin (finalist). His new poetry manuscript is *Fort Necessity*. He teaches at Georgetown.

Reginald Gibbons is the author of nine books of poems, including *Creatures of a Day* (Louisiana State University Press, 2008) which was a finalist for the National Book Award), and *Slow Trains Overhead* (University of Chicago Press, 2010); a novel, *Sweetbitter* (Louisiana State University Press, 2003); translations of Sophocles and Euripides and of Spanish and Mexican poets; and a book about poetry, *How Poems Think* (University of Chicago Press, 2015). He has taught at the MFA Program for Writers at Warren Wilson College, and is the Frances Hooper Professor of Arts and Humanities at Northwestern University.

Doreen Gildroy is the author of *The Little Field of Self* (University of Chicago Press, 2002), which was winner of the John C. Zacharis First Book Award from *Ploughshares,* and *Human Love* (University of Chicago Pressm, 2005). Her poems have also appeared in *The American Poetry Review, Slate, TriQuarterly,* and elsewhere. She currently is writing a column for *APR* on Poetry and Mysticism.

Jennifer Grotz's third book of poems, *Window Left Open,* appeared from Graywolf Press in 2016. She is director of the Bread Loaf Translators' Conference.

Mark Halliday teaches at Ohio University. His sixth book of poems, *Thresherphobe,* was published in 2013 by the University of Chicago Press. His poem "Blue Spruce" appeared in *Ploughshares* Volume 5, Issue 2 in 1978.

Sarah C. Harwell is the author of the collection *Sit Down Traveler* (Antilever Press, 2012) and, with Courtney Queeney and Farah Marklevits, *Three New Poets* (Sheep Meadow Press, 2006). Currently she works as Associate Director of the MFA Program at Syracuse University.

Robert Hass is the author, most recently, of *What Light Can Do* (essays)

(Ecco, 2013) and *The Apple Trees at Olema* (poems) (Ecco, 2011). He teaches English at the University of California at Berkeley.

Brooks Haxton teaches at the MFA programs of Syracuse University and Warren Wilson College. His most recent books are *Fading Hearts on the River* (Counterpoint, 2015), an account of his son's career in professional poker, and *My Blue Piano* (Syracuse University Press, 2015), a selection of poems translated from the German of Else Lasker-Schüler. His next book, *Mr. Toebones*, will contain original poems and translations.

Seamus Heaney was born in County Derry in Northern Ireland. *Death of a Naturalist*, his first collection of poems, appeared in 1966, and was followed by poetry, criticism, and translations which established him as the leading poet of his generation. In 1995 he was awarded the Nobel Prize in Literature, and twice won the Whitbread Book of the Year, for *The Spirit Level* (1996) and *Beowulf* (1999). *Stepping Stones*, a book of interviews conducted by Dennis O'Driscoll, appeared in 2008; *Human Chain*, his last volume of poems, was awarded the 2010 Forward Prize for Best Collection. He died in 2013.

Tony Hoagland's newest book of poems, *Application for Release from the Dream,* was published by Graywolf Press in 2015. His second and most recent collection of essays about poetry is *Twenty Poems That Could Save America and Other Essays* (Graywolf, 2014). He teaches at the University of Houston.

James Hoch is the author of *Miscreants* and *A Parade of Hands* (W. W. Norton, 2008). He lives in Garrison, NY, and teaches at Ramapo College of New Jersey and Sarah Lawrence.

David Hutcheson received his MFA in poetry in 2014 from Hunter College, where he also taught introductory courses in creative writing. Lately, he has had jobs as a metalworker and freelance editor. He lives in North Carolina.

Mary Karr is the author of *New York Times* bestselling *Art of Memoir* (Harper Collins, 2015) and three award-winning, bestselling memoirs: *The Liars' Club* (Penguin, 2005), *Cherry* (Penguin, 2001), and *Lit* (Harper Perennial, 2010). The most recent of her four poetry books is *Sinners Welcome* (Harper Perennial, 2009). She was a Guggenheim Fellow in poetry. Other grants include the Whiting Writers' Award, PEN's Martha Albrand Award, and Radcliffe's Bunting Fellowship. The Peck Professor of Literature at Syracuse University, she is currently adapting her books for a Showtime series based on her life, starring Mary-Louise Parker.

Christopher Kennedy is the author of four collections of poetry, most recently *Ennui Prophet* (BOA Editions, Ltd., 2011) and *Encouragement for a Man Falling to His Death* (BOA Editions, Ltd., 2007), which received the Isabella Gardner Poetry Award. His work has appeared recently in *Plume, Juked, Ampersand Review, Heavy Feather Review,* and *The Laurel Review.* A recipient of a poetry fellowship from the NEA in 2011, he teaches at Syracuse University where he directs the MFA Program in Creative Writing.

John Kleiner teaches at Williams College. He is the author of *Mismapping the Underworld: Daring and Error in Dante's Comedy* (Stanford University Press, 1994).

Taylor Koekkoek lives in Baltimore where he teaches creative writing at Johns Hopkins University. His stories have appeared in *Tin House* online, *Neon* magazine, and elsewhere.

Philip Levine (1928-2015) is the author of twenty-one books of poetry, most recently *News of the World* (Random House, 2009). He was recipient of the Pulitzer Prize and the National Book Award, and served as chair of the Literature Panel of the National Endowment for the Arts. He was elected a Chancellor of The Academy of American Poets in 2000, and was named the 18th US Poet Laureate by the Library of Congress.

Maurice Manning's next book of poetry, *One Man's Dark*, is forthcoming from Copper Canyon. He lives in Kentucky and teaches at Transylvania University and in the MFA Program for Writers at Warren Wilson College.

Kathryn Maris, a poet from New York now living in London, is the author of *God Loves You* (Seren, 2013) and *The Book of Jobs* (Four Way Books, 2006). She was a Fellow at the Fine Arts Work Center in Provincetown, and her poems have appeared in *Granta, The Poetry Review, Poetry London, Poetry, The Nation, The Fi-*

nancial Times, as well as anthologies including *Best British Poetry* and *The Pushcart Prize Anthology.* She teaches at the Poetry School in London.

David Tomas Martinez's debut collection of poetry, *Hustle*, was released in 2014 by Sarabande Books. It won the New England Book Festival's prize in poetry, the Devil's Kitchen Reading Award, and honorable mention in the Antonio Cisneros Del Moral Prize. He is the 2015 winner of the Verlaine Poetry Prize from Inprint. Currently, Martinez is Visiting Assistant Professor in creative writing at Texas Tech.

Donna Masini is the author of *Turning to Fiction* (W. W. Norton, 2004) and *That Kind of Danger* (Beacon Press, 1994), which won the Barnard Women Poets Prize; and the novel *About Yvonne* (W. W. Norton 1998). Her work has appeared in *Open City, The Paris Review, APR, Parnassus, Boulevard, Cortland Review, Best American Poetry 2015,* and other publications. A recipient of NEA and NYFA Grants, she is a professor of English at Hunter College. She has recently completed a novel, *The Good Enough Mother.*

Jamaal May's poetry explores the tension between opposites to render a sonically rich argument for the interconnectivity of people, worlds, and ideas. He is the author of *Hum* (Alice James Books, 2013) and *The Big Book of Exit Strategies* (Alice James Books, 20016), as well as the recipient of several honors, including a Lannan Foundation grant, American Library Association's Notable Book Award, the Spirit of Detroit Award, the Wood

Prize from *Poetry*, and a fellowship from the Civitella Ranieri Foundation. Jamaal codirects OW! Arts with Tarfia Faizullah.

Nathan McClain is the author of *Scale* (Four Way Books, 2017). His poems have recently appeared or are forthcoming in *Iron Horse Literary Review*, *Southern Humanities Review*, *Waxwing*, *New Haven Review*, and *The Volta*. A recipient of scholarships from The Frost Place and the Bread Loaf Writers' Conference, Nathan is also a graduate of Warren Wilson's MFA Program for Writers and a Cave Canem fellow. He currently lives and works in Brooklyn.

Michael McFee has taught poetry writing at UNC-Chapel Hill since 1990. He is the author of ten books of poetry—most recently *That Was Oasis* (Carnegie Mellon University Press, 2012), a full-length collection, and *The Smallest Talk* (Bull City Press, 2007), a chapbook of one-line poems—and his second collection of essays, *Appointed Rounds*, is forthcoming from Mercer University Press. In 2009, he received the James Still Award for Writing about the Appalachian South, from the Fellowship of Southern Writers.

James McMichael's most recent book of poems, *Capacity* (Farrar, Straus and Giroux, 2006), was a finalist for the National Book Award in 2006. His new book, *If You Can Tell*, was published by Farrar, Straus and Giroux in February 2016. Among his awards are a Guggenheim Fellowship, a Whiting Writers' Award, The Arthur O. Rense Prize from the American Academy of

Arts and Letters, The Shelley Memorial Prize, and an Academy of American Poets Fellowship.

Christopher Merrill's recent books include *Boat* (poetry) (Tupelo Press, 2013), *Necessities* (prose poetry) (White Pine Press, 2013), and *The Tree of the Doves: Ceremony, Expedition, War* (nonfiction) (Milkweed Editions, 2011). He directs the International Writing Program at the University of Iowa.

Joseph Millar is the author of three collections, most recently *Blue Rust*, from Carnegie-Mellon in 2012. His poetry has won fellowships from the NEA and the Guggenheim Foundation. He teaches in Pacific University's low residency MFA.

Carol Moldaw is the author of one novel, *The Widening* (Etruscan Press, 2008), and five books of poetry including, most recently, *So Late, So Soon: New and Selected Poems* (Etruscan Press, 2010) and *The Lightning Field* (Oberlin College Press, 2003), which won the 2002 FIELD Poetry Prize. New work has recently been published in *Denver Quarterly*, *Plume*, and *Sou'wester*. Her new book of poems, *Beauty, Refracted,* is forthcoming from Four Way Books in the winter of 2018. Moldaw lives in Santa Fe, NM, with her husband and daughter. carolmoldaw.com

Honor Moore's most recent collection is *Red Shoes* (W.W. Norton & Company, 2005), and her memoir, *The Bishop's Daughter* (W.W. Norton & Company, 2008), was a finalist for the National Book Critics Circle award. New poems have appeared in the inaugural issue of *Freeman's* and the *New York Times*. In progress are a book about her mother and a new collection of poems; she's also co-editing Writing Women's Liberation for the Library of America.

Tomás Q. Morín is the author of the poetry collection *A Larger Country* (American Poetry Review, 2012), winner of the APR/Honickman Prize, and translator of Pablo Neruda's *The Heights of Macchu Picchu* (Copper Canyon Press, 2014). He is coeditor with Mari L'Esperance of *Coming Close: Forty Essays on Philip Levine* (Prairie Lights Books, 2013). He teaches at Texas State University and in the low residency MFA program of Vermont College of Fine Arts.

Michael Morse is the author of *Void and Compensation* (Canarium Books, 2015). He lives in Brooklyn, NY, and teaches at the Ethical Culture Fieldston School, the Iowa Summer Writing Festival, and the summer workshops at the Fine Arts Work Center in Provincetown.

John Murillo is the author of the poetry collection, *Up Jump the Boogie*, finalist for both the Kate Tufts Discovery Award and the Pen Open Book Award. His honors include a Pushcart Prize and fellowships from the National Endowment for the Arts, the Bread Loaf Writers Conference, Fine Arts Work Center in Provincetown, Cave Canem Foundation, and the Wisconsin Institute for Creative Writing. He teaches at Hampshire College and New York University.

Sharon Olds has published twelve collections including *Satan Says* (University of Pittsburgh Press, 1980), *The Dead and The Living* (Knopf, 1984), *The Wellspring* (Knopf, 1996) and *Stag's Leap* (Knopf, 2013), which won both the Pulitzer and T.S. Eliot Prizes. Olds was New York State Poet Laureate 1998-2000 and is currently a professor at New York University. Her newest book, *Odes,* will be out in Fall 2016.

Soraya Palmer hails from Brooklyn, NY, with roots in Trinidad and Jamaica. She recently completed her MFA in fiction from Virginia Tech, where she taught writing and coordinated a mentoring program for girls. Her prose has been published in *Callaloo, Black Warrior Review, and Calyx,* and she has work forthcoming in *Ninth Letter.* The enclosed story is part of her novel in progress.

Katie Peterson's most recent books are *The Accounts and Permission*. She teaches at UC Davis. She works in video, photo, bookmaking, and sculpture with her husband Young Suh, and their first collaborative exhibition, "Can We Live Here? Stories from a Difficult World" showed at Mills College in Oakland, California from January 20 to March 16th of this year.

Emilia Phillips is the author of two poetry collections, *Signaletics* (University of Akron Press, 2013) and *Groundspeed* (University of Akron Press, 2016), and three chapbooks. Her poems and lyric essays appear in *Agni, Boston Review, Gulf Coast, Harvard Review, The Kenyon Review, Narrative, New England Review, Ninth Letter, Poetry,* and elsewhere. She is the Assistant Professor of Creative Writing at Centenary College of New Jersey, poetry faculty for the Tinker Mountain Writers' Workshop, and the interviews editor for *32 Poems*.

Patrick Phillips' third collection, *Elegy for a Broken Machine*, was a finalist for the 2015 National Book Award. He is also the author of *Boy and Chattahoochee*, which won the Kate Tufts Discovery Award. His nonfiction book *Blood at the Root: A Lynching, A Racial Cleansing, and the Hidden History of Home* is forthcoming in 2016 from W. W. Norton. Phillips lives in Brooklyn and teaches at Drew University.

Robert Pinsky's recent books are his *Selected Poems* (Farrar, Straus and Giroux, 2011) and the anthology *Singing School* (W. W. Norton, 2014). His albums with Grammy-winning pianist Laurence Hobgood are *PoemJazz* (Circumstantial Productions, 2012) and *HouseHour* (Circumstantial Productions, 2015). As US Poet Laureate (1997-2000), Pinsky founded the Favorite Poem Project: thousands of Americans reading aloud and commenting on poems by Emily Dickinson, Walt Whitman, Langston Hughes, Shakespeare, and others, with a growing video library at favoritepoem.org. His new book of poems, forthcoming in October, is *At the Foundling Hospital* (Farrar, Straus and Giroux, 2016).

Stanley Plumly's most recent collection is *Orphan Hours* (W. W. Norton, 2012). His *The Immortal Evening: A Legendary Dinner with Keats,*

Wordsworth, and Lamb (W. W. Norton, 2014) won the Truman Capote Prize for Literary Criticism this past year. He is a Distinguished University Professor at the University of Maryland, College Park.

Robert Polito's most recent books are the poetry collections *Hollywood & God* (University of Chicago Press, 2009) and *Farber on Film* (Library of America, 2009). The former president of the Poetry Foundation, he is Professor of Writing at the New School.

Paisley Rekdal is the author of a book of essays, *The Night My Mother Met Bruce Lee* (Vintage, 2002); a hybrid-genre photo-text memoir that combines poetry, fiction, nonfiction, and photography entitled *Intimate* (Tupelo Press, 2012); and four books of poetry: *A Crash of Rhinos* (University of Georgia Press, 2000), *Six Girls Without Pants* (Eastern Washington University, 2002), *The Invention of the Kaleidoscope* (University of Pittsburgh Press, 2007), and *Animal Eye* (University of Pittsburgh Press, 2012), which was a finalist for the 2013 Kingsley Tufts Prize and the Balcones Prize and winner of the UNT Rilke Prize. Her work has received the Amy Lowell Poetry Traveling Fellowship, a Guggenheim Fellowship, NEA Fellowship, two Pushcart Prizes, a Fulbright Fellowship, and various state arts council awards.

Maurice Riordan's latest collection of poems is *The Water Stealer* (Faber and Faber, 2013). Among his previous collections are *The Holy Land* (Faber and Faber, 2007), *Floods* (Faber and Faber, 2000), and *A Word from the Loki* (Faber and Faber, 1995). He has edited several anthologies, including *The Finest Music: Early Irish Lyrics* (Faber and Faber, 2014) and *A Quark for Mister Mark: 101 Poems about Science* (Faber and Faber, 2000). Born in Lisgoold, Co. Cork, Ireland, he lives in London, where he is editor of *The Poetry Review*.

David Rivard's new book of poems, *Standoff*, will appear from Graywolf in August 2016. His five other books include *Otherwise Elsewhere* (Graywolf Press, 2010), *Sugartown* (Graywolf Press, 2005), and *Wise Poison* (Graywolf Press, 1996), winner of the James Laughlin Prize from the Academy of American Poets and a finalist for the Los Angeles Times Book Award. A recipient of awards from the Guggenheim Foundation, Civitella Ranieri, and the NEA, he teaches in the MFA in Writing program at the University of New Hampshire.

J. Allyn Rosser's fourth book, *Mimi's Trapeze*, appeared in 2014 from the University of Pittsburgh Press. Her previous collection of poems, *Foiled Again* (Ivan R. Dee, 2007), won the New Criterion Poetry Prize in 2007. She has received numerous other awards for her work, among them the J. Howard and Barbara M. J. Wood Prize from *Poetry* and fellowships from the Guggenheim Foundation, the Lannan Foundation, the National Endowment for the Arts, and the Ohio State Arts Council. She teaches at Ohio University.

Michael Ryan has published five books of poems, a collection of essays, an autobiography, and a memoir. Five of the books were *New York Times* Notable Books of the year. The autobiography was reviewed on the front page of *The New York Times Book Review*, and the memoir was excerpted in *The New Yorker*. His poetry has won many awards, including the Lenore Marshall Prize and the Kingsley Tufts Poetry Award. *Guy Novel* will be published in July 2016 by Permanent Press.

Thomas Sayers Ellis is a poet and photographer. He is the author of *The Maverick Room* (Graywolf Press, 2005) and *Skin, Inc.: Identity Repair Poems* (Graywolf Press, 2010). Poems have recently appeared in *The Paris Review*, *Poetry*, *Tin House*, and *The Best American Poetry 2015*. Last year, he was awarded a Guggenheim Fellowship and Heroes Are Gang Leaders, the band of poets and musicians he cofounded, released *The Avant-Age Garde I AMs of the Gal Luxury* (Fast Speaking Music, 2015). TSE is currently a Visiting Writer at The Iowa Writers' Workshop.

Helen Schulman is the author of the novels *This Beautiful Life* (an international bestseller) (Harper, 2011), *A Day at the Beach* (Mariner Books, 2008), *P.S.* (Bloomsbury Publishing PLC, 2002), *The Revisionist* (Crown, 1998), and *Out of Time* (Atheneum, 1991) and the short-story collection *Not a Free Show* (Knopf, 1988). She coedited, along with Jill Bialosky, the anthology *Wanting A Child* (Farrar, Straus and Giroux, 1999). Her fiction and nonfiction have appeared in such places as *Vanity Fair, Time, Vogue, GQ, The New York Times Book Review,* and *The Paris Review.* She is currently the Fiction Coordinator at The Writing Program at The New School, where she is a tenured professor of writing.

Lloyd Schwartz is the Frederick S. Troy Professor of English and teaches in the MFA Program at UMass Boston. His books include *Cairo Traffic* (University of Chicago Press, 2000), *Elizabeth Bishop: Poems, Prose, and Letters* (The Library of America, 2008), and the centennial edition of Bishop's *Prose* (Farrar, Straus and Giroux, 2011). His poems have been chosen for *The Pushcart Prize, The Best American Poetry,* and *The Best of the Best American Poetry.* A Pulitzer Prize-winning critic, his reviews for NPR's *Fresh Air* are collected in *Music In—and On—the Air* (Arrowsmith and PFP, 2013).

Nicole Sealey was born in St. Thomas, USVI, and raised in Apopka, Florida. She is a Cave Canem graduate fellow and the recipient of an Elizabeth George Foundation Grant. She is the author of *The Animal After Whom Other Animals Are Named,* winner of the 2015 Drinking Gourd Chapbook Poetry Prize, forthcoming from Northwestern University Press. Her other honors include an Emerge-Surface-Be Fellowship from the Poetry Project, the Stanley Kunitz Memorial Prize from *The American Poetry Review,* a Daniel Varoujan Award, and the Poetry International Prize. Her work has appeared in *Best New Poets, Copper Nickel, Third Coast,* and else-

where. Nicole holds an MLA in Africana Studies from the University of South Florida and an MFA in creative writing from New York University. She is the Programs Director at Cave Canem Foundation.

Richard Sime earned an MFA in fiction from Sarah Lawrence in 1994, but he's been writing poetry since 2000, when he began attending the Fine Arts Work Center in Provincetown every summer. His work has appeared in *The New Republic, Barrow Street, Salamander, American Arts Quarterly, Provincetown Arts, Passager,* and *Sixfold.* Born in Bremerton, Wash., and raised in North Dakota, he has lived in NYC for fifty years, currently on the bank of the Hudson in the Bronx with his beloved Welsh terrier, Jocki.

Lynn Sloan is the author of the novel *Principles of Navigation* (Fomite, 2015). Her stories have appeared in *American Literary Review, American Fiction Vol. 13, The Literary Review,* and *Nimrod,* among other publications. She has a master's degree in fine art photography.

Bruce Smith was born and raised in Philadelphia, Pa. He is the author of six books of poems, most recently, *Devotions* (University of Chicago Press, 2011), a finalist for the National Book Awards, the National Book Critics Circle Awards, the LA Times Book Award, and the winner of the William Carlos Williams Prize.

Jason Sommer is the author of four poetry collections, the most recent of which, *The Laughter of Adam and*

Eve (Southern Illinois University Press, 2013), won the Crab Orchard Review Prize. He is a collaborative translator, with Hongling Zhang, of works of fiction from China by Wang Xiaobo—*Wang in Love and Bondage* (SUNY Press, 2008)—and Tie Ning—*The Bathing Women* (Scribner, 2014), which was a longlisted finalist for the Man Asian Literary Prize. He has been the recipient of a Whiting Foundation Fellowship.

Piotr Sommer is the author of *Continued* (Wesleyan University Press, 2005) and *Overdoing It* (Hobart and William Smith Colleges Press, 2013). His collected poems, *Po Ciemku Tez (Also in the Dark)* (Wydawnictwo Wojewódzkiej Biblioteki Publicznej i Centrum Animacji Kultury, 2013), appeared in Poland.

Arthur Sze's latest book of poetry, *Compass Rose* (Copper Canyon, 2014), was a finalist for the Pulitzer Prize. *Pig's Heaven Inn*, a bilingual selected poems, was published in Beijing (Intellectual Property Publishing House, 2014). He has received a Jackson Poetry Prize, a Lannan Literary Award, and a Guggenheim Fellowship. A professor emeritus at the Institute of American Indian Arts, as well as a chancellor of the Academy of American Poets, he lives in Santa Fe, NM.

Rosanna Warren teaches in the Committee on Social Thought at the University of Chicago. Her most recent book of poems is *Ghost in a Red Hat* (W. W. Norton, 2012).

Joshua Weiner is the editor of *At the Barriers: On the Poetry of Thom Gunn* (Chicago, 2009), and the author of three books of poetry, *The World's Room* (Chicago 2001), *From the Book of Giants* (Chicago 2006), and *The Figure of a Man Being Swallowed by a Fish* (Chicago 2013).

C. K. Williams' (1936-2015) recent books are *Selected Later Poems* (Farrar, Straus and Giroux, 2015), *All At Once: Prose Poems* (Farrar, Straus and Giroux, 2014), and *Writers Writing Dying* (Farrar Straus and Giroux, 2012). He was a member of the American Academy of Arts and Letters, and taught in the Creative Writing Program at Princeton University.

David Wojahn's most recent books are *World Tree* (Pittsburgh, 2011), which was the winner of the Academy of American Poets' Lenore Marshall Prize, and *From the Valley of Making: Essays on the Craft of Poetry* (University of Michigan Press, 2015). He teaches at Virginia Commonwealth University and in the MFA in Writing Program of the Vermont College of Fine Arts.

Dean Young's most recent book is *Shock by Shock* (Copper Canyon Press, 2015). He currently teaches at the University of Texas, Austin.

GUEST EDITOR POLICY

Ploughshares is published three times a year: mixed issues of poetry and prose in the spring and winter and a prose issue in the summer. The spring and summer issues are guest-edited by different writers of prominence, and winter issues are staff-edited. Guest editors are invited to solicit up to half of their issues, with the other half selected from unsolicited manuscripts screened for them by staff editors. This guest editor policy is designed to introduce readers to different literary circles and tastes, and to offer a fuller representation of the range and diversity of contemporary letters than would be possible with a single editorship. Yet, at the same time, we expect every issue to reflect our overall standards of literary excellence.

SUBMISSION POLICIES

We welcome unsolicited manuscripts from June 1 to January 15 (postmark dates). We also accept submissions online. Please see our website (pshares.org/submit) for more information and guidelines. All submissions postmarked from January 16 to May 31 will be recycled or returned unread. From March 1 to May 15, we accept submissions online for our Emerging Writer's Contest.

Our backlog is unpredictable, and staff editors ultimately have the responsibility of determining for which editor a work is most appropriate. If a manuscript is not timely for one issue, it will be considered for another. Unsolicited work sent directly to a guest editor's home or office will be ignored and discarded.

All mailed manuscripts and correspondence regarding submissions should be accompanied by a self-addressed, stamped envelope (s.a.s.e.) and email address. Expect three to five months for a decision. We now receive well over a thousand manuscripts a month.

For stories and essays that are significantly longer than 6,000 words, we are now accepting submissions for Ploughshares Solos, which will be published as e-books. Pieces for this series, which can be either fiction or nonfiction, can stretch to novella length and range from 7,500 to 25,000 words. The series is edited by Ladette Randolph, *Ploughshares* Editor-in-Chief.

Simultaneous submissions are amenable as long as they are indicated as such and we are notified immediately upon acceptance elsewhere. We do not reprint previously published work. Translations are welcome if permission has been granted. We cannot be responsible for delay, loss, or damage. Payment is upon publication: $25/ printed page, $50 minimum and $250 maximum per author, with two copies of the issue and a one-year subscription. For Ploughshares Solos, payment is $250 for long stories and $500 for work that is closer to a novella. The prize for our Emerging Writer's Contest is $1,000 for the winner in each genre: Fiction, Poetry, and Nonfiction.